Brazilian Jiu-Jitsu

Submission Grappling

TECHNIQUES

Brazilian Jiu-Jitsu

Submission Grappling

TECHNIQUES

Royler Gracie

with
Kid Peligro

Photographs by
Ricardo Azoury

INVISIBLE CITIES PRESS • MONTPELIER, VERMONT

Invisible Cities Press
50 State Street
Montpelier, VT 05602
www.invisiblecitiespress.com

Library of Congress Cataloging-in-Publication Data

Gracie, Royler.
Brazilian jiu-jitsu : submission grappling techniques / Royler Gracie
with Kid Peligro ; photographs by Ricardo Azoury.
p.   cm.
ISBN 1-931229-29-5
1. Jiu-jitsu—Brazil. 2. Self-defense. I. Peligro, Kid. II. Title.
GV1114.G77 2003
796.815'0981—dc22
2003016842

Anyone practicing the techniques in this book does so at his or her own
risk. The authors and the publisher assume no responsibility for the use or
misuse of information contained in this book or for any injuries that may
occur as a result of practicing the techniques contained herein. The illus-
trations and text are for informational purposes only. It is imperative to
practice these holds and techniques under the strict supervision of a qualified instructor. Additionally, one should consult a physician before
embarking on any demanding physical activity.

Book design by Peter Holm, Sterling Hill Productions

Contents

Introduction:
What Is Submission Grappling?

Submission grappling is a meeting of grappling styles. Although no-gi styles of fighting have been around for thousands of years, the modern era of submission grappling began in 1998 with the first Abu Dhabi Combat Club World Submission Wrestling Tournament. The creation of Sheik Tahnoon Bin Zayed Al Nahyan, of the United Arab Emirates, the ADCC captured the imagination and the attention of grappling stylists around the world because of its rich monetary prizes, its exotic location, and especially because of its revolutionary set of rules that awarded value to techniques from most grappling arts.

Why was this so revolutionary? Because, though Brazilian jiu-jitsu had come to dominate the grappling and no-holds-barred worlds through its expansive ground game and submission holds, even it had become

Dancing with joy, Royler celebrates another title, ADCC 2000.
Ricardo Azoury photo

constrained by artificial rules. The ADCC, and the evolution of submission grappling, was a way to return fighting to its essence: a battle of two combatants to determine who would prevail through physical prowess and technical mastery.

The ADCC rules rewarded not only jiu-jitsu moves but also gave a great number of points for takedowns and opened up the gamut of acceptable submission techniques.

Unlike jiu-jitsu competitions, the ADCC allowed most types of foot and leg locks and most other submissions except for neck and spinal cranks. Prior to the ADCC, jiu-jitsu competitors shied away from straight foot locks, considering them cheap shots, and were even booed by spectators if they used them in competition. Most other types of foot and leg locks were illegal. However, after just five years of the ADCC's influence, the artificiality of these rules has become apparent, and not only are foot and leg locks legal but they have forced a serious evolution in the sport, with many new techniques and defenses being developed.

Today, submission grappling events are common in Brazil, the United States, Europe, Japan, and throughout the world. And the ADCC has become the proving ground where top grapplers from different countries and backgrounds find out who is truly number one. I had conquered the world in Brazilian jiu-jitsu, but was eager to find out how I stacked up against the best in other disciplines. That challenge is what first drew me to the ADCC in 1999. It was an invigorating experience, and I came to love the fast and furious action typical of submission grappling matches on my way to three consecutive ADCC titles. It is this love of the sport, along with the techniques that helped me master it, that I hope to convey to you in this book.

For my father, Helio Gracie, whose teachings, advice, and inspiration have made me what I am today, and for my wife, Vera, and my four princesses, Rayna, Rayssa, Rhauani, and Rarine, who give me their unconditional love and support every day.

I owe a debt of gratitude to Ricardo Alvarez and Ron Bergum for the support they have given to me, jiu-jitsu, and the grappling arts over the years. To my longtime friend Kid Peligro, thanks for your friendship, encouragement, and wisdom. I also want to thank David Adiv and Wellington "Megaton" Dias, my loyal friends who represent my work in America, and Ricardo Azoury for his photographic work and friendship. And special thanks to all the people who practice, participate in, and foster the evolution of jiu-jitsu and the grappling arts throughout the world.

The Order of the Positions

Since the release of *Brazilian Jiu-Jitsu: Theory and Technique,* which I created with my cousin Renzo, one of the most common questions I have been asked is, "Why did you decide on those techniques and why did you present them in that order?" Of course, deciding was no easy task, because in Brazilian jiu-jitsu there are so many positions and they are all very important. We could have chosen many new and advanced positions and bedazzled everyone with our knowledge. We could have shown the latest, greatest sweeps that are being used in competition, or the new submissions being taught at the academies in Rio. But we chose not to. I conduct seminars all over the world and am exposed to a large number of students from different cultures, and what I've noticed is that the problem for the average student learning jiu-jitsu today is not learning the latest and greatest, it is learning the basic positions. There aren't enough qualified instructors out there, so many students are on their own to learn the basics properly.

Nowhere to run. Royler applies the final choke on Martin Brown on the way to his unprecedented third consecutive ADCC title, ADCC 2001. Mike McNeil/ADCC News photo

For that book, we decided to select a sampling of the techniques that we felt would benefit beginning students, while at the same time being useful as a reference guide to all practitioners, even the ones lucky enough to have good instructors. We presented a variety of the most commonly used positions in Brazilian jiu-jitsu. We also tried to sequence them, for the most part, according to the order we teach in regular classes. Generally, no one learns three or four sweeps or takedowns in a class; classes are structured so that the student learns certain moves that eventually interconnect and develop into a complete game.

When I am teaching a new student at the Gracie Humaita Academy, in the first lesson I will teach one sweep, one submission, and one escape. The next lesson, I will teach perhaps another submission, a takedown, and another escape. I have to build my student into a fighter, and the best way to do that is to slowly start giving him the tools to fight.

If I show you four different sweeps the first day, and then four more sweeps the next day, even if they are related, all you will be able to see are sweeps. You will be confused about when and why you use each of them. But if I have only shown you one sweep, when we fall into a certain position, the only option in your mind will be that sweep. If you only know one submission, when the times comes for you to use it, I know that you won't be wasting precious milliseconds debating which submission to use and why. You learn to instantly recognize the moment and the way to apply a certain technique. Once I am satisfied that you know it and have the right decision-making process for its utilization, then—and only then—will I add another similar tool to your arsenal. This teaching technique was developed and perfected by my father, brothers, uncles, cousins, and myself as the best way for a student to assimilate the information.

Additionally, if all you know are eight sweeps, then we cannot spar, because you don't know how to pass the guard, how to escape from the mount, or how to submit. Each day, I give you a few pieces of the puzzle that can be connected and expanded into a game. I can show you twenty sweeps in a three-week period and nothing else, and you may become a sweeps master, but at the end of three weeks you still can't spar, and if I pit you against another student who has learned the positions in the correct order, he will submit you every time.

For this book, I faced the same questions. And again, in choosing the order of the positions, I have drawn on my decades of experience in teaching, along with my relatives' teachings. But I have diverged from the pattern used in my first book, which was an introductory text.

Since this is a book about submission grappling, however, I have assumed that you have a basis in some grappling art. I assume that you have trained for at least a couple of years and know the basics of defense and attacks, including sweeps, guard passes, and submissions. For that reason, I have not set up the positions in the order that I teach them, but instead have grouped them together by type as much as possible. This offers the advanced student a few benefits. If you want to add a sweep to your game, you can flip through the related sweeps and decide which is right for you. You can also compare similar positions, which are grouped together, and start to pick up on the subtle differences between them and the changes in circumstance that cause you to switch from one to another.

In addition to paying great attention to the order of the positions in this book, I've had to choose which positions to include. I didn't want to just show a collection of super-advanced techniques, because the more advanced a technique is, the less useful it is. The most advanced techniques are developed for a very specific situation, so they rarely come into play. The techniques presented in this book are the ones that you can and will use most of the time in a submission grappling match. They naturally combine to make a complete game. Learn them well and you will have no significant weaknesses.

How-to books almost always mention how no book can ever take the place of a qualified instructor. While that is certainly true, I want to add a caveat to that. The great thing a book does have is pictures showing the *exact* position one should be in to make a technique work. If you study the details of the pictures *very* closely, together with the written explanations, you will certainly be able to learn the techniques completely.

When learning techniques from this book, start with the motion and the general instruction, but as you begin to truly understand the position, go back and examine the pictures closely. Note my hand position, foot placement, and weight distribution. Pay attention to the grips I use and how I align my hips with my head. The text is important for ideas, guidance, and essential details, but at some point more words can only obscure what the pictures already show perfectly. I have gone to great effort to make the best possible pictures that show the correct details and angles. Study them, along with the explanations, and you will have the essence of my technique.

Gi Training

Agreat number of people fighting submission grappling come from a martial art that uses the gi. I strongly recommend that everyone who is going to learn submission grappling train with a gi before taking the gi off. There are many reasons for this. The gi makes you more technical because it forces you to concentrate on the details and posture. In jiu-jitsu, for example, you begin wearing a gi, learning self-defense, learning how to escape from being mounted, and so on. There is a program and progress. Then, once you attain a certain level of proficiency, take off the gi, and start to train submission grappling, you find it easy to adapt your techniques to the lack of a gi. However, if the opposite occurs—you learn to train without the gi and then someday need to fight with a gi—you will have great difficulty dealing with your opponent's level of control over you.

The overwhelming success of Brazilian jiu-jitsu fighters in competitions such as the ADCC, Grapplers Quest, Arnolds, and NAGA is the best proof for training with a gi. (From 1998 to 2001, 75 percent of the ADCC winners were from jiu-jitsu backgrounds.) Since your opponent can grab the sleeves and collar of your gi, you must constantly be in proper posture and be always mindful of your neck and arms; this develops great awareness of the game. The gi also demands a lot more precision, and therefore makes you a better fighter. The gi offers a greater variety of holds, submissions, and options for sweeps. With the gi, you must develop an acute sense of balance and, most important, a great defense. Because you are dry, you have to anticipate your escapes and be more precise with your defenses.

The basic gi course requires a person to participate from six months to two years to start to fully understand the game. I believe that after one year you can start to go without the gi and practice submission grappling, because by then you know the basics and understand what is happening in the training.

Of course, if you never train without the gi, you will have a hard time when you finally do it. You will miss the "handles" and the grips. You will especially miss a variety of chokes and uses for the sleeves and collars. So definitely train without a gi for a while before any big submission grappling competition.

I train with a gi most of the time. If I am going to compete in NHB or

ADCC, then I shed the gi a month or so in advance. I trained jiu-jitsu for thirty-four years and only took off the gi in 1996 when I fought in the Vale-Tudo Open in Japan, which was my first vale-tudo outside of Brazil. From then on I started to practice regularly without the gi and began to perfect a series of adjustments to the style and the techniques that I had learned, so they would be deadly effective in submission grappling. It is those techniques that make up this book.

Surrounded by His Highnesses Sheiks Tahnoon and Hazza Bin Zayed al Nahyan, Royler hoists his first winner's trophy, ADCC 1999. Sussi Dahl photo

The No-Gi Game

If you have never trained without a gi before, you are in for a great new challenge. The no-gi game is different, no doubt about it. Because you don't have a gi to control your opponent and keep him dry, submission grappling is a game of speed and quickness of thinking that requires more out of its participant in many ways. Your physical abilities will be tested to the fullest because you are much more able to move from position to position and can match up against a more technical fighter and still prevail. This downplaying of technique turns some people off, but if you are looking for a pure form of combat, this is just the ticket. Submission grappling prepares you for the real thing.

In submission grappling, you have to make better use of your grips. In fact, you have to develop a whole new set of grips. The wrist, the back of the neck, the ankle, the knee, the elbow—these are all different grips than their jiu-jitsu counterparts. The main thing about no-gi fighting is that it's slippery. Without the gi to grip, many times you lose your holds. The trick is not to be too set on a particular plan. With a gi, you can proceed one step at a time and be pretty certain where you are going next. Without the gi, you can't be so determined to control a certain grip. You have to let things happen, flow with the situation.

Because it is seemingly a less technical game, to be successful in submission grappling you also absolutely must make the best use of your body. For instance, in the open guard, my feet work like hands, gripping my opponent's biceps as they follow his arm movement, keeping contact with him. When going for an arm bar from the guard, my legs climb on my opponent's back, keeping him from moving away from me. I use my heels like hands again, cupping and digging his back to keep extra control. I need to make use of my weight, applying it to the correct points to take away the opponent's ability to just slip away.

Additionally, instead of only thinking one step ahead, now you have to think three or four steps ahead because things happen so quickly due to the nature of the sport. The grips slip, so you lose and regain your grip a lot more. Sometimes you grab and lose, then grab and lose again. You need to be prepared to take advantage of the times you do get control, and not to get discouraged when you lose control, because that happens to everyone constantly in submission grappling. The real key is being ready for your opponent's escape. Not that you plan on failure, but having your contingency plan in place—anticipating where he is going to escape to and how he is going to escape—can get you far. What ways can he escape? How does he usually like to escape? Once you know that, you can have the next attack ready to go and can shorten the gap. Because if he is late on the first one, he will likely fall further behind on the second and third attacks, and that is what you need to succeed.

This may sound contradictory, but in submission grappling the grips, because they are less efficient, actually become more important than in gi training. With the gi, you have a great variety of grips; in submission grappling there are only a few that work with any degree of efficiency, so they each become more important.

How do you compensate for this lack of control? One way is by distributing your weight better on your opponent, but again, sometimes it is hard to apply pressure and use your weight effectively in submission grappling because when you are both sweaty, things become very slippery. To compensate for that you need to be quicker and tighter. You need to train to be "there," to be tight, to be in effect glued to your opponent so you can follow his every move and make your speed and quickness of thinking and reacting your best ally for controlling him.

Controlling the hips is one of the keys to passing the guard. Royler fights for control against Baret Yoshida in the finals of ADCC 2001. Mike McNeil/ADCC News photo

The adjustments need to be faster and more precise than in gi training. You need to be one step ahead or better yet two steps ahead. Timing becomes of great importance because with quicker reactions and sharper timing you will be able to follow your opponent's movements and stay close to his body and in effect use that to control him. Timing is the best way to achieve this because most of the time you cannot control a position and try to hold it, as you would with a gi. It's worth noting that submission training will also help your gi game, because it will sharpen your every reflex.

A good analogy is driving a car. If you are driving down the road and a rock falls in front of your car, you instinctively step on the brakes, swerve, and avoid it. If you have to stop and think, you will hit the rock. In submission grappling your reaction patterns need to be automatic as well. You learn to subconsciously project into the future and to have alternative plans in case that future surprises you.

This doesn't mean that you are going to just be jumping and moving all the time in submission grappling. It means you should be doing the adjustments, small or large, faster and more efficiently than your opponent. At times, in fact, doing nothing may be the best option. For instance, say your opponent is trying to sweep you and has you completely off balance. Sometimes you are so late that the best option is to just lay there like dead weight, let him make his move, and hope that he gives you a chance to regain your balance. Adjusting quickly doesn't mean just flopping around. It means adjusting whatever needs to be adjusted—be that body position, grip, or weight distribution—to keep your advantage and be one step ahead of the opponent.

Passing the Guard

The key to passing the guard in submission grappling is to be in a position where you don't *have* to pass the guard. In every position you can think of, the ideal is to position yourself in such a way that you can't be submitted, and the guard is no different. So the first thing you need to do before you begin to think about passing the guard is to adjust yourself and do a check to make sure nothing is out of place. Is my neck safe? Is my back straight? Is my head erect in relation to my torso, not pointing down? Are my elbows tight against my body and inside his legs? Does my opponent have control of my wrists or elbows or arms? If so, you must go back to step one and make certain that everything is safe.

Every attacking move you make—whether it is a submission attempt, an attempt to pass the guard, or even a sweep—becomes a danger spot for you as well, because it leaves an opening for a counter. If you proceed forward, you will give him a chance to submit you.

Once you are certain you can't be submitted, your next step is to make sure you have proper base and won't be swept or reversed. Check your posture and positioning in relation to the opponent and assure yourself that you have enough control of the position. Are you in good base and not leaning too far forward or back? Does your opponent have any hooks that are effective? Once that is established, then proceed with the pass. Passing is generally accomplished by either controlling or deflecting your opponent's hips. In the control method, you take away his hip mobility and therefore his ability to create space; you are halfway to passing. Then it is just a matter of methodically advancing around the obstacles, in this case legs and arms, until you get across-side. In the deflection method, you take away the power of the hips and legs by deflecting the hips away, pushing the hips or legs to one side, and passing by the opposite side.

When you end up in someone's guard and you are trying to pass, passing should not be your first concern, but rather one of the last. Adjust everything correctly before you go forward!

All this can happen in a matter of seconds or less. With practice and quickness of thinking, these adjustments should be done automatically. You shouldn't even be aware of these things; as you progress and gain skill, your subconscious will do them for you. Anyone advanced enough to be training submission grappling should be surveying every situation that they find themselves in and comparing it to the scenarios they have learned in class or competition over the years, seeing what tools they have that fit best.

Once you achieve a position, you want to maintain it. For example, if you reach across-side and immediately start trying to submit your opponent, you stand a bigger chance of losing the position. Then all that work getting across the side was for nothing. Every position is very important and must be given the proper respect. One's ability to keep a position is a measure of one's progress. Once you are sure about keeping the position, you should begin surveying the situation and seeing what opportunities are available. Can you get an arm, is there an opening for a mount, or should you go for his foot? The best part about this order of movement and strategy is that by simply maintaining the position, you force the opponent to do something in order to escape. Once he tries to escape, he will have to expose himself, and then it is time for the kill.

Defending the Guard

The same basic strategy applies to defending the guard in submission grappling as to attacking it. When I am on my back and have the opponent in my guard, what should be my first objective? Avoiding a submission! In submission grappling, the opponent trying to pass my guard can best submit me with foot or leg locks. Unlike in jiu-jitsu, where the gi makes it easy to defend a foot lock, in submission grappling your foot is exposed when you have someone in your guard. So my first priority is to make certain that he can't get my foot. Preventing him from passing my guard is actually my second objective. No sense in defending the guard and giving him my foot for a submission!

You have a few ways to protect your foot in the guard. The first and best is to maintain closed guard, keeping your feet crossed behind your opponent's back. That will certainly make it difficult for him to get your foot in a submission. A variety of attacks can be used from the closed guard not only to prevent your opponent from opening it but also to further advance your position or have a quick end to the match: the guillotine, the kimura, and sweeps like the crossover. If he avoids these maneuvers and forces you to open the guard, then you have to "hide" your feet. Anytime you leave one of your feet outside his knees, you run the risk of a foot lock. You must immediately put both feet inside his knees, which can be accomplished by using the "hooks inside." This also takes away the leg-lock option. Sometimes you can't do this because you were late or some other positional reason. In that case, you must control your opponent's head by holding the back of his neck and his elbows, preventing him from going back for the foot lock.

Once you have protected your feet, you can take action to prevent him from passing you. Whenever I defend the guard, I try to put myself in an advantageous position. I like to do an "arm-drag" and slip to his back, but in case that doesn't work I need to have options to deter his progress. I try to give my opponent reasons to take steps back and become defensive by putting him in some danger of a submission or a sweep. I might attempt a guillotine choke or a sweep, or I can try to hook my leg around his for a foot lock.

But if all that has been tried and he is still advancing, then you need to regain position. In all defensive actions, one of the best elements you can have is distance. An example of distance as a defensive tactic is a defense force being attacked by an army. The army has guns that can reach three miles, so what is the best course of defense? Stay at least three and a half miles away! Similarly, whenever you are defending the guard, "distance" is the best option most of the time. Your opponent can't pass your guard if he can't get close to you!

That may seem simplistic, but it isn't. Every time your opponent is getting close to you, putting his weight on you, grabbing and controlling your legs or hips, the first thing you should look for is space. You need to somehow re-create that three-and-a-half-mile distance for comfort and security. You accomplish that by escaping your hips, putting a foot on his body and pushing away, or using your arms to push his body away.

This is just one example of the basic doctrine of defense, which is to deny your opponent what he wants as soon as he wants it. Deny him control of the space between the two of you and keep him from controlling your hips. If he can control your hips, then he has taken away your ability to create space and he will pass for sure. Deny your opponent everything that he wants! If he wants to grab your wrist, that is something that he needs to pass and you shouldn't give it to him. If he gets it, you should try to take it back. Of course, timing and execution may be on his side and he may get it and proceed, but if at every stage you concentrate on denying him what he wants, you will make his job a lot harder.

Royler goes for a Kimura, forcing Anthony Hamlett to retreat in his attempt to pass the guard or be forced to tap out, ADCC 1999.
Ricardo Azoury photo

Fighting "Phrases"

Certain positions in submission grappling go together so naturally that I think of them as words linked to form a phrase: the same phrases or sequences pop up again and again. To really learn them, to get as comfortable with them as you are with speech, you must practice and practice and then practice some more.

I can give you a rough guide on how to devise some combinations. For example, the sweep and the arm bar from the guard are neighbors; they live right next door to each other. So you should practice the arm bar, and when your opponent defends by pushing his weight forward, you quickly change to the sweep. Now you have your first combination.

The "omoplata" and the triangle have a similar relation. You attack with the triangle, and when the opponent defends it, he may leave an opening for the omoplata. You switch to that, and then go back and forth: when he postures to defend the triangle by raising his head and trying to bring the arm to the same side of the body, he makes an opening for the omoplata again. Now you have a four-attack sequence to practice! And once you get this sequence down, you really will have a formidable set of weapons.

Do the same thing for other related positions and all of a sudden you have some natural large phrases that are interlinked for a solid game. At the highest level of performance, all the options are connected to one another and the best choice depends on your opponent's position, weaknesses, and similar variables. Now you have some notion of the submission grappling roadmap. As you develop, the roadmap fills in more and more with back roads, shortcuts, loops, blind alleys, and other options. "You can't get there from here!" disappears from your vocabulary. You can always get there.

Training Routine

To compensate for the lack of control in submission grappling, you have to spend a great amount of time training on the mat, learning the nuances and subtleties of the sport. It isn't enough to be in great physical condition, because this is a fast-paced game. You need to sharpen your neuromuscular skills to the greatest degree possible because everything happens very fast in submission grappling, much faster than in other grappling styles, because of the slipperiness factor.

I recommend a lot of agility drills, like calisthenics or plyometrics, anything that can sharpen the mind-body connection so that you react more quickly to what you see.

In addition, you need to learn positions in an order that makes sense. You don't learn an arm lock and a choke at the exact same time. There is a real logic to the way you proceed in learning and progressing in any martial art, and submission grappling is no different. Again, you don't learn an arm lock and a choke at the exact same time, but after a while you learn to use them in sequence. You string them together. First you learn an "upa" (bridge), then you learn how to pass the guard, then you learn about defending an arm lock, and then little by little you learn how to mix the positions.

One thing you learn, once you advance beyond a certain level in submission grappling or jiu-jitsu, is that everyone is able to defend a straight-ahead attack. If you concentrate your efforts on getting an arm lock, your opponent will focus on defending that single attack. In martial arts, as in war, defending is stronger than attacking, and it is easier to defend against someone who is using only one attack. So it is important to mix things up, to string positions together, to use feints to throw your opponent off balance, and to create an element of confusion.

How do you learn to achieve this? As you learn positions and start to master them, you will naturally start to piece your game together. First, you put two techniques together. From there, make a conscious effort to add a third one. Eventually, you'll have the tools to deal with a particular situation. Always start with the techniques you are most comfortable with, because those are usually the ones that will succeed most frequently. Even when they don't succeed, they will create enough "reaction" that something else opens up. If you start with the ones you don't do well, or try something that you are not comfortable with, then you may just give your opponent such an opening.

On the other hand, there is a use for those moves you don't do so well. You don't want to really try them, but they are perfect for feints, to clear the way for the move you really want to spring. In general, it is important to learn a variety of things and then sort out what works for you because the more options you have in your arsenal the harder it will be for your opponent to keep countering you.

Picture your opponent as a house with ten windows and three doors, and you want to get into it. It doesn't matter if you get in through a window or a door, so long as you get in.

Royler attacks Robson Moura's foot during the semifinals of ADCC 2000.
Gustavo Aragao photo

Initially, you have the door on the right opening and closing several times and the left window also opens and closes several times. Are you able to react quickly enough to take advantage of these openings? Sometimes all the windows are open but the doors are closed, and sometimes it's the other way around. But at any time, in any position, there are a number of openings and choices that are available, and it is the fighter with the greatest precision, the fastest reaction, and the quickest thinking who will get into that house. It is fundamental for a fighter to have this kind of fast mental reaction on both defense and offense, which entails having options in place two or three moves ahead.

With each new move, the entire house changes. An opponent putting a hook inside your legs slams shut the front door, but pops open the attic window. You have to know the house so well that you recognize what has changed instantly. You can't sit back comparing mental pictures and trying to figure out what's changed.

Developing a Complete Game

A frequent question I'm asked in the seminars I conduct is, "How do you develop a complete game?" My answer is that you need to do two things, neither of which people like to hear much. Make sure you can fight well on both sides, and work on the *weakest* aspects of your game.

The Two-Sided Game

Most people generally develop a one-sided game. They prefer to pass the guard to one side and defend the guard to one side, and their sweeps are generally also one-sided. Yet when you see a top-notch grappler compete, one of the things that strikes you is his ability to do things to both sides. It seems almost effortless. Of course, nothing is further from the truth. The top guys reach a two-sided game by practicing much more than regular students. The demands of competing against different opponents with different tendencies force them to develop both sides or fail.

Does this mean all black belts are ambidextrous? Certainly not. Many have an Achilles' heel that they try to keep hidden. If they possess a very strong game with a certain characteristic, they will, most of the time, dictate the direction that the training will go and avoid having to go to their weak side. The problem arises when they are faced with a superior opponent who forces things to go to the other side.

Having said that, I don't recommend that you practice both sides equally from the beginning. I never did, and I don't encourage anyone do that in my school. The best way to develop your game to both sides is to first fully develop your better side. Completely understanding the moves and the details to your favorite side is a must. Once you have this knowledge down and are confident with it, then you should slowly "transfer" that knowledge to the other side.

I have used this method with great success, and it is what I teach my students. I have found that your conscious and subconscious will absorb this sequence of instruction better than if you try to develop both sides at once.

Many times, injuries will force you to accelerate this process and develop the weaker side or a different part of your game. Perhaps you twisted an ankle and can't use the hook to that side, and that forces you to sweep the other way or use a different sweep than you normally do. Or you hurt your elbow and have to attack the neck with the other arm or pull to the opposite side. Even if you don't become somewhat ambidextrous by your own choosing, eventually you may be forced by circumstances beyond your control to learn to use both sides.

Once you have mastered a move to one side, one of the best ways to become equally adept from the other side is to get a partner of equal size and technical level and simply practice drills to your bad side. If your triangle is good to the right, do ten to that side and twenty to the left. The important thing is not to get ahead of yourself. If you can't do something really well to one side, that is okay. Improve your strong side to the point that you feel it is close to perfect, then try to duplicate the results on the other side.

Improving Your Weaknesses

Another common sight is the student who has a few moves that he likes and avoids the other parts of the game, concentrating on further improving what he does and likes best. Sometimes such students are able to channel the sparring to their favorite positions, but you can't count on that. If you want to see great improvement in your game in a short period of time, you must concentrate on improving the weakest part of it. Of course, it is more fun to concentrate on what you do best. If you like passing the guard and being on top, it is easy and even rewarding to continue to perfect that while avoiding being on that bottom that you hate so much. The same thing goes for the guard players; it is much more fun to refine that spider guard sweep combination than to try to be on top and learn to pass. But you will never develop an effective and complete game that way.

When I teach my students, I have a system to help them work on their weaknesses. In the beginning, I let them develop what they like to do and concentrate on that. If a student likes to fight from the bottom, I let him get comfortable with that and enjoy the feel of training, but after a while I start to practice the stuff that he doesn't like. If the guy likes to play the guard, he will naturally pull guard and play guard. I don't have to force him to do that. What I try to do is to reverse the game and force him to play from the top. That has two functions. Playing on the top, he becomes comfortable with other aspects of the game, such as passing the guard, maintaining good posture, avoiding submissions, developing good base to avoid sweeps, and so on. Additionally, since he is now trying to play the top, he will see the game from the opposite perspective. When he tries to pass, he learns what he needs to do to pass and what the opponent does to counter his moves, so when he reverts back to the bottom, he will know what the top guy is looking for and how he thinks, which will improve both sides of his game.

In terms of improvement, working on the weaker parts of your game will pay off much more than continuing to work on what you already do well. It is far more difficult to improve what you are already great at another 10 percent than to improve something you are not so good at. And even if you do, it probably won't make that much difference in competition—you already do it well! But when you practice the worst part of your game, it's easy to improve 30 percent, and that 30 percent will be a huge difference in your training and competing. You will have entirely eliminated a weakness.

Think of a triathlete who is very strong at swimming. He may dedicate a great amount of time to practicing his swimming, but this will only cut 5 percent off his time and that will shave maybe fifteen seconds off his total time. But if he is weak at running and he concentrates on improving running, he may be able to easily cut his time by 15 percent, and that 15 percent might mean cutting several minutes off his total time. By working on his weakness, he gets a much greater overall improvement with the same effort.

Creating Your Training Family

I had the incredible luck to be brought up in the Gracie family. Ever since I was a child, I have been exposed to an inordinate amount of technical knowledge and ring talk. The conversation at the table always revolved around fighting, strategy, technique, mental preparation, and so on. My father, uncles, and brothers always shared their knowledge freely, so the household was a living classroom every day.

Growing up, I trained a lot with Rolls, my brother who died in a hang-gliding accident. I mirrored his game a lot. His game was always going forward, very aggressive, very fast. I spent much of my youth around him, and he helped me both technically and strategically. Later on, I trained with Rickson, and Rickson helped expand other areas of my life, like discipline, the mental part of fighting, the ability to be calm during matches. Eventually, I developed my own set of rules, techniques, and strategies, which is what I share with my students and now with you, the readers of this book.

Since most of you are not born into a large family of fighters, it is important for you to create your own "family" of training partners. You should find a good school, with a good instructor, and make that into your "family." Your instructor should guide you and share his knowledge with you. You and your partners should try to do the same.

An important consideration, if this is going to be your training family, is that you need to be sure that you feel good being there. You need to be happy going to the academy. An instructor should be aware of that and must try to make his academy a great place to be, where the instructors are looking after the students, are happy teaching, and transmit their joy in their teaching. He must make sure that the techniques and instruction are state of the art. Once you have that kind of environment, then it is up to you to really want to be there and make it into your family. If you feel like the academy is your second home, you are more likely to enjoy learning there.

Your relationship with your instructor can make or break your grappling experience. I'm certainly very conscious of that, so I try to do everything I can to make my students' experience as positive and beneficial as possible.

I have my own style of teaching. In a private lesson, I'll teach my student a technique or set of techniques and then we spar. At that point, I lower my level of sparring to your level and try simulate a person with similar understanding and execution as you, but at the same time I'll get you to repeat the same position over and over without you really thinking about it. I simply direct the training to repeat the same technique in different situations. At the same time, I'll correct any minor mistakes you are making; for instance, if your hand is in the wrong place, I'll grab it and move it to the right place without you even noticing. Or if your foot is not pushing where it should be, I'll adjust it without telling you, so you get the right feel of the position. Soon, you're placing your hands and feet in exactly the right location.

I try to customize a specific curriculum to meet each of my students' needs. In group classes where this is not possible, I divide the class into different levels, especially if there are a lot of beginners or a lot of black belts. I then teach a series of techniques that are relevant to what we have seen before and slightly progress every week or every month. Because the sport is always progressing, I have to keep adding new techniques to keep my students and myself up to date.

In a group class, I still try to correct each individual as needed. With advanced students, I can go into a lot of detail; whereas, with blue belts, I concentrate on the generalities. I don't want them to get too focused on fine details; otherwise, they may lose the big picture and not learn to use the technique properly. Often, the beginner or young intermediate fighter is so determined to get the finest points of a certain technique that he ends up not knowing the when's, the why's, and the how's. There is a time for and a point to everything. If you are learning to swim, the first thing you need to do is learn to float. Then maybe you learn a stroke, and then you practice. But if I come to you just when you are learning to float, and I say, "you know, in the freestyle, you need to keep your little finger bent at 85 degrees to get proper flow in the water," then I'm not doing you any favors.

Choosing Your Training Partner

Choosing who you train with can greatly affect your progress in submission grappling. You should select someone with similar goals. If you just love submission grappling and want to do it to get in shape and learn how to move, you need to train with people that are more like you. Imagine, for instance, that you are a surgeon and you train with all of the toughest guys at the academy, and then one day you break your hand! Maybe you can't work for a month, maybe your hand never heals properly. If you want to have fun and practice the sport for personal enjoyment, choose people that are seeking the same objective.

If, on the other hand, you want to compete at world-class levels, like the ADCC World Submission Wrestling Championships, then you need to train with competitive, advanced, determined fighters. That still doesn't

Royler attacks Baret Yoshida's foot while attempting to pass the guard with the knee through the left, ADCC 2000. Ricardo Azoury photo

mean you should train with reckless people. Before a competition, I have to stay healthy and injury free, so the closer it gets to the competition, the fewer training partners I throw into the mix. I don't want to get injured at the last minute and throw all my hard work out the window!

I usually have one "hard" training session in the morning and an easier, skill-sharpening session in the afternoon. The hard training session will be against one of my toughest *(but still not reckless)* sparring partners, who will simulate my opponent. The easy session will be against a guy that I find easier to catch in submissions. He will still be very skilled but perhaps plays a more open game and makes a few more mistakes. I use this person to fine-tune all the moves that I have acquired and to work on sharpening the timing and precision of the moves.

Any time you are developing a new position, start out practicing against a less skilled, lighter opponent, preferably a beginner with some knowledge of the sport. Since he is not at your level and preferably not as strong, you will be able to sharpen the move and repeat the move with a certain frequency, because you will control the sparring match. As you get confident with the move, you should move up to a heavier training partner but maintain the skill level. Once you have the move down pat, then you should begin to try it with the more advanced fighters and the heavier fighters. As you practice the position following this pattern, what happens is you begin to adjust and adapt the position to your body type and style. At that point, you should have acquired the speed and perfected the dynamics and nuances of the position well enough that you can use it against a fighter of any skill level and size.

Don't start by trying a move you haven't got completely figured out against someone of equal or greater skill. You will probably fail, and you may not get the chance to repeat the move the entire training. Then you may not want to use it again because you think it doesn't work, but the truth is that it never had a chance. Say you are beginning to learn to dunk a basketball and you go one-on-one with Michael Jordan. What should you expect? He is going to stuff the ball down your throat and then you are going to say, "I can't dunk!" But the truth is that you may be able to dunk; you just chose the wrong partner!

Getting out of a Rut

Generally speaking, as you get a series of techniques or a specific game down, you tend to be more effective and your results improve. You have greater and greater success with the same moves and the moves get sharper and sharper. You start to feel really good about your game! However, you aren't training with a dummy but rather with another human being who is intelligent and very capable of recognizing what you are doing and adapting his defenses. Soon, what was very successful doesn't work and you are forced to change, to learn new tricks. But change doesn't always come quickly; it takes time to incorporate the new moves into your game, and sometimes you fall into a rut.

As you learn new techniques and begin to implement them, your timing naturally will be less sharp. After all, these things are new to you and they take time to fit into your game. At the same time, you stop using your tried-and-true techniques because you are concentrating on your new ones. They aren't working anymore, and now you're stuck in no man's land. You don't have the new weapons ready yet, your game loses its sharpness, you get frustrated and feel like quitting. How do you get out of this situation?

My personal experience has been that the quickest way to get out of one of these ruts is to practice the new moves over and over with a willing partner. Repetition will help you get the timing of the technique and also let you understand the subtle nuances of each move until you have a full understanding of what you are doing and how to accomplish it. The next step, for me, is to start training with lighter, lower-level practitioners in the academy. I can repeat the same positions over and over, without the fear that one mistake will cost me dearly. If you try to practice your new game against someone more advanced than you, chances are that it won't work and you'll just give up and go back to the old.

Another great thing you can do is take time off. In my experience, I have found that time away from the mat lets your mind ease off the pressure to progress. The pressure and frustration of adjusting to a new game sometimes make it even more difficult to sort the moves out and to have the clear thinking necessary for fast reactions. Once you come back refreshed, you'll be able to focus on the game again.

Injuries

I am a very energetic person and am on the go all the time. I wake up early, teach privates all morning, then work out in the middle of the day before returning to the academy in the afternoon for more privates and group lessons.

The risk, however, is that when you are on the go all the time, you don't allow your body to recover and this pace eventually causes injuries. Over the years, I have learned that one of the most important things you can do is to allow your body and mind to rest. The natural tendency is to simply ignore the body's messages. Most of the time, however, something eventually gives and you are "forced" to rest and recuperate.

I liken it to driving a car and the oil light goes on. Rather than stopping and adding the oil, you simply ignore the warning light and continue to drive. At some point, the car will break down and force you to stop. Whether you are a high-level competitor or just an enthusiastic practitioner, it is very important to rest properly. Grappling is a very demanding sport. It requires a lot from your body and your mind. If you always train and do not rest properly, you will likely get injured. Something will give and, rather than rest a little, your body will force you to rest a lot. Don't want to take a day off? Your body may say, "Here's a pulled hamstring, buddy. Take four weeks off!"

Grappling is not a sport that you need to train for every day all day. In fact, some of my top students prefer to train only a few days a week—except of course when competition nears. I personally like to train all the time, but even I have had to understand the demands of my body and adjust my routine accordingly.

If you are a serious grappler, even if you take steps to protect your body as much as possible, there will come a time when you get injured. I have been training and competing in jiu-jitsu, submission grappling, and vale-tudo fighting for more than thirty years. Over those years, I have sustained my share of injuries and have been around a number of students who got injured. Injuries are a part of the sport, but how you deal with them and what you do during that time may help or hinder your development as a practitioner.

The first step to take when confronted with an injury is to stop training and assess the nature and extent of the damage. Many times, you can do that yourself for lighter injuries, but most of the time you should consult a specialist to fully determine not only the extent of the injury but also the proper course of action.

Having taken those steps, it is up to you to make the best of the situation. Don't get down on yourself or start feeling miserable. Thoughts like, "Bad things always happen to me!" will lead you nowhere except down, so stay away from them and get busy getting better. Injuries take time to heal and a positive attitude will go a long way to make the recuperation seem faster and easier. Start doing the things you can do to help yourself. Improve your overall flexibility, strengthen other areas of your body, or work on your endurance.

For example, when I am injured and can't train, I try to exercise in a way that doesn't aggravate my injury but still maintains my level of fitness. I usually ride my bike on long rides to increase my endurance and burn some of that energy. If I can, I go surfing and release more energy while relaxing and exercising at the same time.

A very important part of the recuperation process is to remain mentally sharp. Watching competition and instructional videos will help enhance your knowledge and keep your mind sharp. Going to the academy and watching classes and other people training will also help keep

Royler using the knee-through pass in the opening round of ADCC 2001.
Mike McNeil/ADCC News photo

your mind in the game. All these suggestions are an important part of everyday progress, but they become even more important when you are injured and can't train.

Ultimately, the best thing to do when injured is to figure out how you got injured and take steps to prevent it from happening again. If you got injured because you trained while tired, take note and learn to rest. If it was because you were practicing against a much bigger person than you, take note. Try not to repeat the same mistakes so that you can stay injury free and enjoy the benefits of submission grappling.

Becoming a Champion

So you want to become a submission grappling champion, but you don't know where to start? Becoming a champion is no easy task; many attempt it, but only a few succeed. I like to say that some champions are born and some champions are made. You must be born with a certain amount of natural talent and inner fire, but lots of people have those qualities and never become champions. It takes a tremendous amount of dedication, an incredible amount of preparation, and long, arduous training sessions. Do you think you have that kind of commitment? And how can you tell?

Look at the competitors you know. There are many reasons why some people always win while others only come close. Many people enter tournaments just for the experience or camaraderie of it. Their goal may be winning one match or finishing in the top five. They don't expect to win, and they aren't disappointed when they don't.

Third time is the charm! An exuberant Royler celebrates his third ADCC World Title in 2001.
Mike McNeil/ADCC News photo

There are some competitors, however, who enter tournaments to win at all costs. They strive to become the champion, and everything else is meaningless. If they end up in second, they feel that they lost! I am one of those, and that desire to compete has led me to some great challenges. A lot of people ask me why I fight guys so much bigger than me. Why don't I concentrate on fighting people in my weight division? The answer is that I constantly need to test myself. I was born into a family of fighters. My father before me, my brothers, uncles, and cousins all fought, whether in vale-tudo, NHB, or jiu-jitsu tournaments. I was one of the youngest, so I've been fighting bigger guys since I was three! We were always competing among ourselves—who was getting better, who was sweeping whom, and so on. I always wanted to be better than the rest and to defeat anyone that I faced, and I still do.

But as I started to win all the tournaments in my weight class, I had to look elsewhere for meaningful challenges. I began entering the Absolute divisions in tournaments, whether an NHB fight or a jiu-jitsu match against much larger opponents, to test myself against the best. I fight these guys to push my limits and to learn.

If you recognize yourself in this description, if you think you are one of those with the drive and will to become a champion, then you must commit yourself to the task. Winning is like everything else; it takes practice. The more events you compete in, the better you get at competing, and the more you'll start to win. That is the first part of your commitment: to compete more often. The second part of the commitment is that when you compete, you commit yourself to winning! Once you do that, everything you do has a purpose. You lift weights harder, run faster, and train longer hours. This involves some sacrifices. In the past, I have rented an apartment and left my house so that I could concentrate 100 percent on training for an event. That, of course, is really hard because I love my family and I miss them. But that is what I believe it takes to win. Preparation is the key to being the best. Without that, you go nowhere. So first, let's look at what goes into a champion's training regimen.

Training

I once read, "Winning happens away from the limelight and the public eye. It happens in the darkness and solitude of the training gym. It happens alone in the long hours of roadwork and preparation." And I fully believe that. You will never become a champion if you don't have the commitment to train harder and longer than the others. You need to have the stamina to perform at your best level for an entire tournament. Otherwise, you may win a match or two, then fade before the finals. So you must do your workouts to improve your cardio, your strength, and your stamina.

Training is a constant in my life. I like to have forty-five days to get ready for a match. I eat well. I bicycle, run, and swim to increase my cardiovascular capacity, and I change my weight-training routine to fit the type of match I am fighting. The only common ground is the aerobic part. After a few minutes on the mat with another champion, endurance becomes a key factor. If you are winded, you won't have the explosive strength needed to make the sudden bursts necessary to achieve a certain move or reverse a position. In the finals of my second world championship, I went against a great young fighter, and early in the fight he scored two points on me via a sweep. At the exact moment that I was being swept, I used my explosiveness to sweep him back and equal the score. Had I not been able to do that right away, and had I let him establish position, the final result could have been very different. But because I was at top fitness level, I was able to do that move, even though it was the finals and I had already fought many difficult matches that day.

I customize my routine to the type of match I'll be fighting. If I am going to be in an NHB match, then I lift weights according to a specific routine set up by my trainer for extra power, and I take supplements according to my nutritionist. I also practice boxing. Many NHB matches come down to quick battles of strength, so that is where I concentrate.

If I'm going to compete in a jiu-jitsu event, then I do a lot of judo and a different series of weight training than I do for NHB. The emphasis is more on endurance than strength.

When I am training for a grappling event, I train much as I would for a jiu-jitsu tournament, but the emphasis once again is different. Grappling is much more slippery than jiu-jitsu and the need is for quick explosive motion, so I adjust my weight training and my cardio accordingly. I may do explosive repetitions with a heavier weight. The important thing to keep in mind is that you need to do your homework and have something that works for you and keep improving it. Fights are won or lost long before you step into the arena.

Cross-training is extremely important in any sport and it is no different in submission grappling. If you want to compete in submission grappling tournaments, you'll obviously need a grappling base, be it in jiu-jitsu, wrestling, judo, or sambo. But once you have that base down, you should cross-train in other martial arts or sports like wrestling. A while back, jiu-jitsu fighters wouldn't train much outside their sport, but that changed with the advent of the ADCC World Submission Wrestling Tournament. The ADCC's very open rules allowed for many different submissions and awarded points for many different throws, so they forced grapplers, especially jiu-jitsu fighters, to open up their eyes and learn other styles. It made them better all-around fighters.

You may say, "Royler, you fight frequently, so why not just stay in tournament condition year-round, instead of gearing up forty-five days ahead of time, then taking a break, then gearing up again?" The truth is that you can't stay in tournament shape year-round. You can be in very good shape all year, but the physical and mental demands are such that you can only achieve peaks so many times during the year. If you try maintain peaks for too long, you'll end up injuring yourself or getting mentally tired and burned out. Listen to your body. If something doesn't feel right, or if you are tired, or some routine is giving you fits, give yourself a break—change your routine. Or rest and change. Do what you need to keep yourself interested.

How do you begin to design your champion training program? The best way is to start with your instructor. Ask him to set up a training regimen for you for the next tournament. Discuss with him what you want to accomplish. Then find a personal trainer or a friend to help you with the sparring.

And don't forget your regular classes. There are many ways you can train, and when you are training to win, you need to pay attention to details. Always be improving something. Every time you train or attend a class, you need to perfect a move, improve your breathing, or adjust a detail. You must always improve, because your opponents are always improving, evolving, and adjusting. So make every training session count. Ask your instructor what you are doing wrong. What points of the game do you need to work on? Ask your training partners the same question. Then ask yourself the same question. When you find out, then you are back on top, ready to do what it takes to win.

Know Yourself

So you are in great shape and technically sound—you're ready to win, right? Not so fast. Before you can regularly win matches, you must know how to compete. Know what to expect—from yourself as well as your opponent. Many top fighters lose because they don't know how to compete. Certainly, you must understand the rules of the event, but there is much more to the mental game than that. For starters, you must be utterly focused on winning. If you compete just for the experience and you are behind in the score, naturally you will try to come back, but if you don't, you aren't crushed. If you want to win always, you must take away from your mind the thought of losing. If you are behind in the score, you know you are going to somehow reverse and win. Even at the last second, you know you are going to do something that will lead to victory. Sometimes, you are so committed that you almost will your opponent into losing.

I can't even tell you how many times this has happened to me. In my three decades of competing, I have been in many matches where everything was stacked against me. I firmly believe that mental commitment carried me to victories in those situations.

There is another aspect to the mental game that isn't often talked about, but it can make or break you as a fighter. Adrenaline. Competition, be it in sports or in life, generates adrenaline—a hormone that triggers the body's "fight or flight" response. Blood pressure goes up, heartbeat increases, blood sugar level rises, your brain becomes super-alert, and blood flow is redirected from digestion and surface areas to muscles and brain. This is a holdover from our animal past, when we needed this extra boost to flee predators and fight rivals. In our everyday struggles on the mats, adrenaline can be felt. But in the increased intensity of a competition, adrenaline becomes a major factor. It affects people differently. The rush makes some perform better. Others seems impervious to its effects, while others seem paralyzed by it. Sometimes, a really good athlete performs way below par in a competition because he cannot deal with the adrenaline rush.

There are three ways to deal with adrenaline. One is to let it overwhelm you, one is to work with it to get the benefits of the rush, and the other is to simply try to ignore it. I like the middle approach. Over the years, I have competed enough times to know what to expect and have become used to the feelings to the point that I only get the benefits. For example, adrenaline is most noticeable at the very beginning of a match, and that can be a good thing. You start tense and defensive, which actually works as a protection mechanism: you risk less and defend more. As the fight progresses, you get more relaxed—and that is when you have to watch out for stupid mistakes.

Some people say that—if you are well prepared physically and mentally—you can avoid the adrenaline stress. Don't believe it. The fact is that you can be a world champion and still react to the pressures of competition. Beginner or expert, featherweight or hulk, when you step inside the four lines, you know the terror. People don't talk about it much, but it is there for all of us. The night before and the week before a competition is a complex time. Only the experiences you have had before will give you an understanding of what is ahead.

Once again, my recommendation is to enter enough competitions to get used to the feeling. Another one is to have people next to you who are mentally strong and will help you overcome the nervousness. When you surround yourself with solid people that you trust, you yourself become stronger.

Obviously, no one starts off as a champion. You have to work your way up. So how do you develop a champion's ability to know himself? I actually recommend that you start competing at the smallest, most local level you can, against the easiest opponents you can find, in order to "learn winning." If you start your competition career in the worlds, you may be in for a shock. The skill level is incredibly high, and you will lose your first matches rather

Foot Locks are a Royler favorite, ADCC 2000. Ricardo Azoury photo

quickly. Then all your effort and preparation go down the drain and discourage you from trying again. So it is important to get some easy matches under your belt in order to develop your game.

Know Your Opponent

Knowing yourself is not enough. You can know yourself through and through, be ultra-fit, and still lose to an inferior opponent who springs one surprise attack on you. The hardest fight for me is one where I fight an opponent that I don't know much about.

Every fighter that does not worry about his opponent's strengths and knowledge enters the match at a serious disadvantage. I like to know who I am fighting and what they like to do. You should watch your opponent fight. In many tournaments, you don't know who all the competitors will be until close to the event, but if you have the chance, you should try to watch them fight. I always try to watch my next opponent's match. If I am in the quarterfinal and I advance, I try to watch the other quarterfinal and study the tendencies of the fighters that I may face.

In the ADCC, for example, you only find out who the fighters are a few days before the event. And the brackets are set the night before the event. When I fought my first ADCC, in 1999, I went in much more blind than I would have liked to—not only because I didn't know all the fighters, but also because I hadn't fought before under these rules and didn't have a chance to develop a thorough fight strategy. I knew I was going to face the best there was from different disciplines in submission grappling. I knew these fighters would be as good or better than I was under these rules, so I trained specifically for those types of situations. I went in there to become champion, but I didn't know what to expect. Everything happened very fast and I was fortunate to win. But I went there with little knowledge about my opponents and without a set strategy in my mind.

After the first ADCC, I began to understand what was expected and what was important to be successful in submission grappling events. I started to organize myself and prepare a little more for that specific situation. No doubt my jiu-jitsu competition background gave me a roadmap to success: the first thing is not to get submitted; then organize yourself, posture, arms, elbows, and so on; then try to pass. One thing at a time. But there were people from different backgrounds launching attacks and reacting in ways that weren't "normal" to me, so the fight was less predictable and the speed of action was a lot faster than in jiu-jitsu competitions.

At the ADCC, we were all in the same boat. It was a new competition, and everybody was more or less unfamiliar. Where you really run into problems is if your opponent knows more about you than you do about him. If you are a skilled fighter and pretty confident in your physical abilities to win, you want to take away as much as possible the element of chance, the possibility of a surprise. No one is foolproof, and even an old, familiar adversary can spring a surprise on you, but in general, if you study your opponent's game and prepare for his reactions and preferences, you will be in good position to win.

If you can, get tapes of your opponent fighting. Study how he likes to pass the guard, what sweeps he prefers, what submissions he likes to use. Also look for his weaknesses. What sweeps does he fall for? If he got submitted, what technique was used? Did he fall for it because he was late or inattentive? If it was because he was late, what caused him to be late? Was it the move before? Or two moves before? Does he have a side he prefers to pass on? Or defend? Try to compile all that and have a mental picture of your opponent going into the fight.

With that picture in mind, try to see what elements in your game best match your opponent's style, what techniques are best suited to each situation. The winner, in general, is not the lucky guy. Most of the time, the winner is the person that can bring the match to his own game. For instance, if you are a sambo fighter, you would like nothing better than to exchange foot and knee locks with your opponent. If you are a pure wrestler, you would have a strategy based on fighting standing. If the fight goes to the ground, you must have a strategy to survive there and to bring the match to standing again. Someone who is very strong at passing the guard will attempt to fight from the top, as opposed to being taken down and having to defend the guard. If he can bring the game to his field of expertise, he will greatly increase his chances of winning. In this case, how does he assure himself of being on top? There are many options, but the best one is to be good at takedowns. He needs to practice wrestling, judo, and jiu-jitsu to add to the takedowns that he already has.

Now, what if you like to be on top but are going to fight against someone who is a better wrestler or better at takedowns than you are? You need to prepare for the contingency that you may end up on the bottom. Since you want to be on top, what do you do? You must be ready to sweep the guy or to slide and be on his back.

Or say you like to play from the bottom. What do you do to prepare for the match? You can just go into the match and pull guard or half-guard and start the match under "your" conditions, but in submission grappling events like the ADCC, especially in the finals, that counts as a negative. So you need to have a strategy or a set of techniques that will get you to the bottom without being scored upon.

These are the sorts of concerns that a champion has on his mind days, even months, before an event. Like I said, becoming a champion is not for the half-hearted.

Winning Strategy

Strategy is a big part of winning. A fight has a beginning, a middle, and an end. All are important. In the beginning phase, you are cautious and look for an advantage. If you are able to get ahead on the score, you are in control of the match. It is up to your opponent to catch up, which forces him to take chances. You must be ready to take advantage of the chances he will take. If you stay ahead into the middle of the fight, you should bring the fight to your environment. Do the things you do best and let your opponent open up. As the fight gets toward the end, your opponent will risk even more, but at this point, you need to be prepared to contain yourself. Many times, risking a submission or a sweep late in the match will give your opponent an opportunity to reverse and score, and you may end up losing the fight. At this point, late in the match and ahead in the score, you must know how much time is left in the match and how large your point lead is. If it is large, you may allow a sweep or a low-scoring move to happen, rather than fight it and expose yourself to a submission. If your lead is narrow, you don't have such a luxury.

If you fall behind on the score in a match, the situation changes. Then it is up to you to open up and take risks. If you are behind early in the match, you can still allow the match to run its course and stay with your original master plan, but you need to have a plan to become more aggressive at a set time. In a ten-minute match, some people are comfortable being behind with three minutes to go, while others start to take chances earlier. Generally speaking, if you have a solid game, you should be able to continue to create situations under your normal pace to even the score. If with three minutes left you are still behind, it is time to take bigger risks. The size of the risks depends on the score spread, but you need to understand your game, your strengths and your limitations, and have a clear picture of what you want to do and where you want to be at every part of the match. Of course, any time a good submission opportunity presents itself you may want to take it, but keep in mind that doing so does open doors for your opponent.

Everyone is different, but by competing frequently and later analyzing the matches and your performance, you will be able to develop your own fight strategy.

Training Goals

We have been talking about the mentality and commitment it takes to become a champion, but I want to make it clear that this isn't the only reason to practice a martial art. Because I've been such an avid competitor, people sometimes think that I force my students to compete.

The truth is that I don't push anyone to compete. As a matter of fact, my school does not have a huge competition team. We do have a quality competition team, but it is certainly not as large as other academies of the same size. We have a large number of students that have never competed and have no interest in it, and that is fine with me.

Martial arts are for everyone. The slow, the fast, the large, the small, the young, the old, the competitors and the noncompetitors—all have a home here. They all have something to gain and something to contribute. If a school is so dedicated to competition that it segregates or ridicules the noncompetitors, then it is limiting access to the sport to the very fit and denying a lot of people the chance to learn a great art.

One advantage to competing is that you participate in more intense training sessions. As the competition nears, the training gets harder and harder and your techniques and timing get sharpened quickly. Needing to score, the competitor has to narrow the scope of his game to put certain moves into practice right away. He experiences bursts of progress brought about by these intense demands.

Where the head goes the body follows. Royler controls the head and arm in his attempt to pass the guard, ADCC 2001.
Gustavo Aragao photo

On the other hand, the regular student generally trains at the same pace every week, so his progress is more steady. You don't learn certain things as fast, but without a specific time frame artificially set by tournament schedules, you can concentrate on the nuances and finesse of every move until you have it down perfectly. Do not concern yourself with winning every training session or whether you got submitted many times in class. Your concern is steady gains. First, develop your defense. Once you have a solid defense, the attacks will come. Once you have the assurance that you can protect yourself in any situation, then your mind is free to look for opportunities for reversals and submissions.

Most of all, if you train for personal gain, make sure you enjoy every training session and always leave the academy with a good feeling. As I like to say, whether you're driving a Ferrari or a VW Bug, if you stick to the right road, you will get to the same destination. And that is all that matters.

Meet the Team

The Authors

Royler Gracie

The time? 1996. The place? Rio de Janeiro. The scene? Gracie Humaita, the academy where Brazilian jiu-jitsu began. It is summer in Rio, and the temperature soars above 104 degrees. Most people in Rio have escaped to the mountains or the beaches, but not the students of Gracie Humaita, and especially not their instructor, Royler Gracie. Instead of dispatching everyone for the waves, Royler closes the windows of the academy and shuts off the fans. The heat is unbearable. "Let's train!" he shouts.

To the aghast students, he says, "You think this is hot? Wait until we

get to Tijuca Tennis Club at noon—then you will see what hot is! Do you guys want to be champions? I do, and this is what it takes to be one. Listen to me and we are going to win!"

That is vintage Royler Gracie, one of the most intense jiu-jitsu practitioners ever to don a gi. Tijuca Tennis Club hosted the first Brazilian Jiu-Jitsu World Championships that year, and Royler's team was ready. Royler entered himself and two other black belts in the featherweight category, and they took the top three positions.

Royler returned to claim another world title in 1997, but wasn't satisfied with just the featherweight title this time. Knowing that a 143-pounder could only go so far in the Absolute division, he still entered, fighting a 275-pounder in the first round. Royler defeated him with ease. He went on to defeat another 200-pounder before finally losing to the equally large world champion in the semifinal. His awe-inspiring performance earned him the Most Technical Fighter award.

Royler doesn't talk about his career record much because he knows it speaks for itself. Four-time World Jiu-Jitsu champion. Three-time ADCC Submission Wrestling champion. Vale Tudo champion. Pan-American champion. Pride 2 champion. Twenty-First-Century Warriors champion. The list goes on and on.

Now closing in on age forty, with a storied career behind him, Royler is still one of the most influential and sought-out teachers in jiu-jitsu. What makes him such a good instructor? His intensity and his will to win are factors, but they come from within and can be hard to translate from instructor to student.

To really understand what makes Royler a superb submission grappling instructor, take a look at that list of Most Technical Fighter awards. Royler has spent much of his career defeating larger—sometimes much larger—men in the ring. To do this, you must be a master of each position, seizing any advantage given you.

The other incredible thing about Royler is that he holds down his duties as academy instructor and top-notch competitor while being father to four daughters. Royler takes his role as father seriously—as he does his surfing hobby and his projects to help needy children in Rio de Janeiro.

Kid Peligro

Kid has been involved in the martial arts for most of his life. He attained the rank of brown belt in American kenpo before discovering Brazilian jiu-jitsu. He earned his black belt in that sport after ten years of practice. In that time, he trained and became friends with some of the best instructors and practitioners in the business, including Rickson, Royler, and Royce Gracie. Being on the cutting edge of the technical developments of the sport and having been involved with the ADCC tournament from the beginning makes Kid the most qualified person to transform Royler's technical knowledge and skills into words. Kid has witnessed hundreds of submission grappling matches around the world, including all ADCC events. He was one of Royler's sparring partners in all of his winning ADCC campaigns, giving him a rare in-depth understanding of the techniques and strategies of the champions.

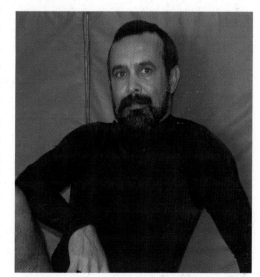

Kid is best known as one of the leading writers in martial arts. He's responsible for regular columns in *Grappling*, *Gracie Magazine*, and *ADCC News*. He is also the author or coauthor of three of the most successful martial arts books in recent years: *The Gracie Way*, *Brazilian Jiu-Jitsu: Theory and Technique*, and *Brazilian Jiu-Jitsu Self-Defense Techniques*.

The Assistants

Helping Royler demonstrate his techniques are two of his top instructors:

David Adiv

David Adiv started his journey into martial arts in his native Israel. David began learning Judo at the age of five and won local, national, and international championships, receiving his black belt at age sixteen. After discovering Brazilian jiu-jitsu in 1990, David started to train under Royler in 1992. David received all his belts from Royler, and was awarded his black belt in 2000.

David accompanied Royler and Rickson Gracie for Royler's first Vale-Tudo match in Japan in 1995 and has traveled with Royler as a training partner and cornerman in every major match since. He has competed in two Pan-American championships, taking second place both times. He also competed in the first Rickson Gracie International Tournament, where he not only won his division, but also walked away with the award for the most technical fighter.

Wellington "Megaton" Dias

Megaton was born and raised in Rio de Janeiro, Brazil, starting his martial arts training when he was five years old. He achieved his judo black belt rank in 1984 and was Rio state champion. While training and competing in judo, Megaton met Royler Gracie. Royler invited him to train at the Gracie Academy. He trained under Royler, Rolker, and Rickson Gracie, eventually receiving his black belt at the age of eighteen from Royler. He has since had the opportunity to train with some of the best Olympic athletes and coaches in the world.

Megaton finished second in the BJJ World Championships in 1995 and third in 1999, 2000, and 2001. He won the Pan-American title in 1998, 2000, and 2001 and was the gold medallist in the Fourth International BJJ Championship in 2002. He also won the Rickson Gracie International Championship in 1997 and 2000, winning the most technical fighter award as well. Megaton lives in Phoenix, Arizona, where he directs the Megaton Brazilian Jiu-Jitsu Academy.

Grips

Gustavo Aragao photo

Because the grips in submission grappling are so different from jiu-jitsu and most other gi-based sports, and because they are so important, Royler will show the proper techniques for the most important ones.

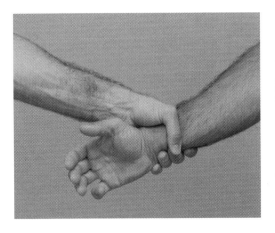

1. Outside wrist grip

Circle your fingers around the opponent's wrist, with your thumb on the inside. Grab the wrist as close to the hand as possible without actually encircling the hand. This grip is good for most types of hand and arm control, as the opponent does not have a way of grabbing your arm back. The weakness is the thumb area, with one finger only, which can be escaped by turning the wrist to the area where the fingers meet the thumb and prying out through there.

2. Double outside wrist grip

This is the same as the outside wrist grip, but with both arms.

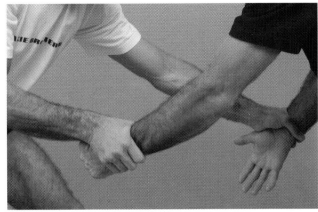

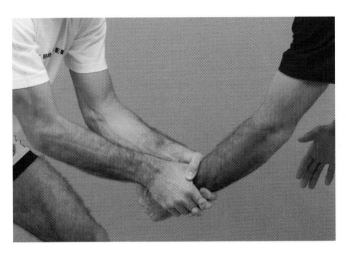

3. Two-handed wrist grip

Both hands grab the wrist, with the fingers and the thumb circling it. Grab as near the hand as possible. This provides great control of the opponent's arm and is good for drags or takedowns.

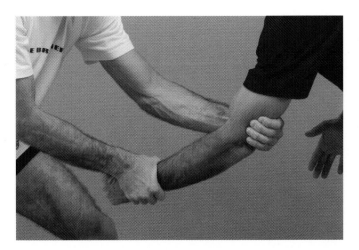

4 Wrist and elbow grip
This is an outside wrist grip combined with an inside elbow grip. Notice that the elbow grip is just above the elbow on the widest area. This is good for arm drags.

5. Neck clinch
Both hands cup the neck area, with the elbows close together. This provides great control of the head and the inside. You can direct the opponent, as his body must follow his head.

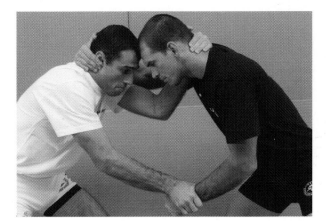

6. Outside wrist grip with single neck grip
Grab the outside of the wrist and the outside of the neck. You still have some advantage over the opponent, as you control his wrist.

7. Hands interlaced

This is a neutral grip, as both fighters have equal control. Be sure to keep a firm wrist, because if the opponent is able to bend your wrist back, you will be forced to go wherever he wants.

8. Collar and elbow clinch

Another neutral grip, this is a very common clinch in the stand-up phase of submission grappling matches. Both fighters cup the outside of the neck and the elbow. Keep pressure on the opponent by pulling down on his neck and elbow.

9. Collar and inside elbow clinch

You control the neck and the inside of the forearm to the same side with your hands. This is useful to break the collar and elbow clinch.

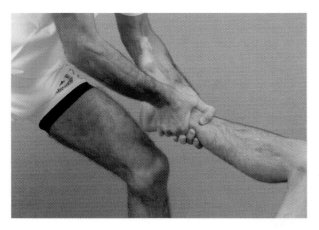

10. Two-handed ankle grip
Both hands grab the ankle as close to the foot as possible. This provides good control of the leg for passing or for throwing the leg to one side.

11. Inside ankle grip
Grab the ankles with each hand on the inside. This is important for guard passing, for throwing the opponent's legs to one side, or for stepping through. It's also good for avoiding the opponent's hooks.

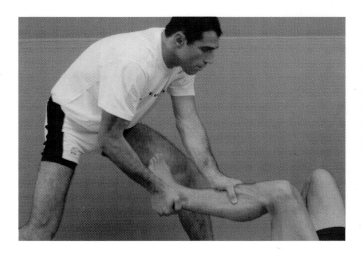

12. Under-the-ankle and shin grip
One hand cups under the ankle and the other grabs the top of the shin of the same leg. This is good for keeping the opponent's back on the mat and preventing him from sitting or standing.

13. Ankle and inside the knee grip
One hand controls the ankle, grabbing it under and outside near the foot, while the other hand grabs the inside of the knee. This affords you great leg control, as you can torque the lower leg, forcing the opponent to turn. It's also a great way to pass the guard: simply push the right hand in, and the left hand blocking the inside of the left knee will force the opponent to give you the right pass, as he must turn his body.

14. Inside wrist grip
This neutral grip is used to keep your opponent from gripping something better.

15. Single-arm grip inside wrist and outside elbow
Grab the inside of the opponent's wrist with one hand and the outside of the same elbow with the other hand. This is commonly used in the open guard to control one arm. The inside wrist grip is neutral, but the outside of the elbow gives you domination of the arm.

16. Behind the ankle and over the knee grip
One hand cups behind the ankle and the other pushes over the knee of the same leg. This is good for guard control and sweeps. It's also a good way to keep the opponent at a distance.

17. Hooks
Your foot goes behind the thigh, knee, or ankle, with the toes curled. This is immensely important in sweeps and open guard work.

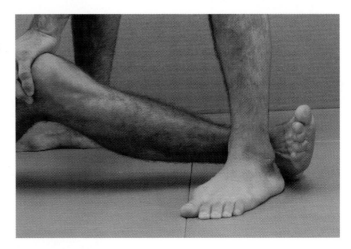

18. Behind the ankle and the knee grip
One hand grabs behind the ankle while the other grabs behind the knee. This provides good leg control to keep the opponent's back on the ground.

19. Double under-the-arms clinch

Each arm goes between the opponent's arm and body, clasping the hands together and cinching the opponent's chest close to your chest for great inside control. This is great for the standing clinch and especially important for butterfly guard sweeps and taking the back. For butterfly guard control, your arms should be as high as possible (close to the armpit).

20. Rear clinch

This can be over one or both arms or no arm at all. Your arms go around the opponent's waist, with one hand grabbing the other wrist to lock the grip. Tightness is extremely important, as any space will allow the opponent to slip his arms inside to break the grip. For best control, the grip should be as close to the hips as possible.

21. Americana or Kimura grip

Wrap your arm around the opponent's arm and lock your wrist with your own hand. This is good for the Kimura but also helps a lot in sweeps.

Drills

Gustavo Aragao photo

Warm-ups are very important. They not only serve as a way to get your muscles loose and avoid injuries, but also are a way to get your neuromuscular system in gear. The first five positions in this book are drills designed to improve your physical performance and execution of the actual techniques. They can be practiced before any training routine and should be done at the beginning of each day of practice.

The hip escape drill is a great way to warm up your body, as it uses most of the muscles and joints in your body while replicating one of the most commonly used motions in submission grappling, the hip escape. Having a "soft" or "flexible" hip is one of the keys to progress in submission grappling. In fact, good hip movement is often used as a way to measure progress. The key to this motion is to bend at the waist. A very common mistake—even among advanced practitioners—is to keep a stiff hip while doing the hip escape.

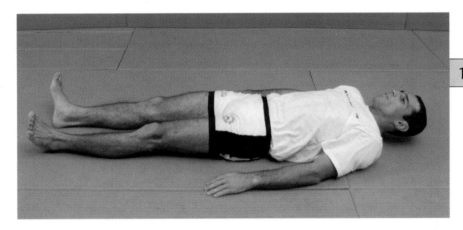

1 Royler starts off lying flat on the mat, arms straight next to his body.

Royler bends his right leg and plants his right foot on the mat. **2**

3 Pushing off his right foot, Royler jack-knifes his hips to his right by pushing his buttocks out while bringing his head toward his knees. This simulates pushing off an opponent with his arms.

Royler curls his left leg in and plants his left foot on the mat. **4**

5 Royler brings his body completely to the neutral position, but this time has his left foot planted and begins the hip escape to the opposite direction.

And repeats the motion to his left, making sure he bends at the waist like a switchblade. **6**

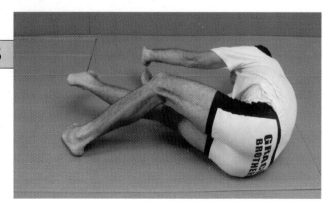

Standing-up-in-base drill

Being able to stand up in base is another very important technique in self-defense, sports jiu-jitsu, and submission grappling. Many times in a match, an opponent will disengage from you and give you the option to stand up. If you stand up without proper technique, the opponent may attack, push you back down, and score points for the takedown. In this second warm-up sequence, Royler "lubricates" his knee and hip joints, along with the shoulders.

1 Royler lays down flat on the mat with his legs bent at the knees and both feet planted on the mat.

Royler sits up, plants his left hand slightly behind him and off to the side, curls up his left leg, and rests his right arm on his right knee. Now Royler has a good base, with his weight equally distributed between his right leg and left arm. **2**

3 Royler pushes off his right foot and left arm and raises his hips, while sliding his left leg through between the gap formed by his right foot and left hand, until he can firmly plant his left foot on the mat in base, slightly behind his body. At this point Royler has a great three-point base with his right foot in front, left foot back, and left hand down. Note that he keeps his knees bent and torso low to his legs. This is very important because it gives him not only base but also the ability to shift his weight to compensate, in case his opponent tries to push or pull him off base.

4 Having ascertained that his opponent is not coming forward to push him, Royler extends his body while remaining alert and in good base.

Repeat this drill at least five times to each side.

3 Walking-in-base drill

The ability to maintain balance is a very basic aspect of any form of fighting. This is especially so in submission grappling, because takedown points are given a great deal of importance and being on the top is such an advantageous position. In this drill, Royler integrates his legs, hips, and arms, along with warming up his neck area. The neck is one of the most important areas in submission grappling, and one of the most neglected. Not only is it vulnerable to submissions, but because so few holds are effective in submission grappling, it is very common for the opponent to control you by holding the back of your neck. This drill not only uses the entire body together, but it also develops base when walking while your opponent is controlling your neck.

1 Royler is in base with his feet firmly planted on the mat, parallel to each other. His knees are bent and his hips are low, helping him maintain his base. Megaton grabs the back of Royler's neck with his left hand as he pulls Royler forward. Royler maintains his base by leading with his neck while keeping his stomach area tight, maintaining muscle connection from his legs to his hips. At first, just develop your balance without any motion.

2 As you begin to warm up and feel your base progressing, start the motion drill. While Megaton maintains the pulling pressure, Royler walks back, leading with his head and pulling Megaton with him.

3 Megaton switches hands and pulls Royler forward as they walk back and forth.

Notice that it is important for Royler to keep his head straight and maintain a straight line with his back all the way to his hips. If you bend at the head, you lose balance and control. "Where the head goes, the body follows!" If you bend at the spine or the back, the same thing will happen. So if you begin to lose your balance and you have to adjust to recover, do it with quick steps while maintaining form with your upper body. **4**

This drill is useful for both positions, so you should alternate with your partner. Not only is the defensive role helpful, but the attacking partner will develop the balance necessary to take advantage of the controlling hold.

Pummeling drill

"He who controls the center controls the position." That motto is never more true than in standing techniques where the person with his arms inside his opponent's armpits controls the middle and thus the entire situation.

In this pummeling drill, Royler not only makes you work your arms, shoulders, hips, and feet, but also makes you practice the invaluable skill of slipping your arms inside for control.

1 Royler starts off facing Megaton in the over-under clinch, with his right arm inside Megaton's left arm, while Megaton has the same position on the other side. Royler begins the exercise in coordination with Megaton by circling his left hand around Megaton's right forearm until he can slide his left arm between Megaton's right arm and body, while Megaton simultaneously does the same move to Royler.

Notice that they both have to work in synchronicity as they exchange arm positions and alternate swinging their shoulders and heads from side to side. **2**

3) The object is to start off slow and warm up, practicing the ability to slip your hands inside your opponent's arms, as if you were swimming.

After you have mastered the move and warmed up, try (4) to see who can be faster than the other and end up with both arms inside.

Detail

Notice the hand position: palm facing in and fingers close together, sliding over the forearm just above the elbow to reach the gap between the arm and the body.

Do the drill for at least three minutes, until you break a sweat. As you begin to gain speed, try to attain the inside position.

5

Takedown drill

In this final warm-up drill, Royler uses a simple motion to take his opponent's back and go for a takedown. Again, Royler uses a simple technique as a warm-up drill in order to make the best use of the warm- up time to practice important moves. Royler likes to use these moves specifically as drills because they are the building blocks of so many advanced moves, and because they provide a complete warm-up.

1 Royler starts off facing Megaton in a collar and elbow clinch. His right hand is behind Megaton's head, controlling the neck, and his left hand is holding Megaton's forearm near the elbow. Megaton has a similar grip on Royler. This is a very common situation in submission grappling.

Royler takes a quick step forward, just past Megaton's body, and quickly pushes Megaton's right elbow up, allowing Royler to dip his head under. (Note that if your opponent has an extremely strong grip on you, you may not be able to free yourself so easily. In that case, refer to position 7.) Royler makes sure he keeps contact, with his head on Megaton's arm, and uses the back of his head to propel Megaton's arm forward with a quick flinch. This not only forces Megaton to lean forward but also prevents him from quickly replacing his arm in front of Royler's face. **2**

3 Royler continues the motion and slides behind Megaton and bear hugs him. Notice Royler's feet position and base, ready to control and accompany Megaton if he moves in any direction. Royler needs to keep his head turned to one side and his head and body tight on Megaton's back, pushing against the back, so that Megaton can't swing his body around and get his arm around Royler's face.

3 Reverse Angle

Notice how Royler's bear hug traps Megaton's arm. This occurs as a consequence of the move, since Royler's right arm was in front of Megaton and his left one circled around the back, looking for the bear hug. This may not happen every time—an opponent may open his arms wide—but it is the ideal situation and should be the way you practice the drill. Also notice Royler's grip, with his left hand clasping his own right wrist for extra control.

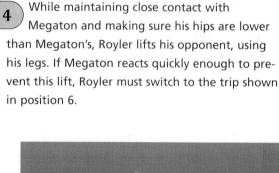

4 While maintaining close contact with Megaton and making sure his hips are lower than Megaton's, Royler lifts his opponent, using his legs. If Megaton reacts quickly enough to prevent this lift, Royler must switch to the trip shown in position 6.

Royler drops Megaton down on **5** the mat, turning him in the air so that he lands on his side and Royler ends up behind him.

Standing Techniques

Gustavo Aragao photo

6

Tripping takedown from the back

In position 5, Royler achieved the bear hug from the back position and went for a lifting throw, as Megaton did not react quickly enough. This time, however, Megaton reacts to the bear hug by opening his legs wide and dropping his hips down, making it difficult for Royler to execute the lifting throw. In this case, Royler must adjust and use a variation of the common trip to take him down. From there, Royler continues the motion to achieve the mounted position.

1 Using the motions described in position 5, Royler has achieved the bear hug from behind, but this time Megaton defends by opening his legs and dropping his hips down.

Royler extends his left leg and plants his left foot right behind Megaton's left heel. Keeping a tight grip on Megaton's waist, Royler switches his right hand to grab around Megaton's left wrist and starts to sit back toward his right heel. **2**

3 As he sits back, Royler torques Megaton back with him. Megaton can't step back with his left leg to regain balance, so he falls to the mat. Notice that Royler still maintains the grip on Megaton's left wrist and uses his own left arm to brace and control his fall to the mat.

Royler continues the twisting/spinning motion, following Megaton to the mat, and throws his right leg over the fallen Megaton.

4

5 Royler continues the motion, achieving the mounted position.

7

Taking the back—strong grip variation

In position 5, Royler got to Megaton's back by simply pushing up his right elbow and sliding around his arm. There are many cases, however, when your opponent will have a firm grip and be putting pressure on your neck as he is pulling down on it, making it very hard to simply push his elbow up and take the back. In that case, you will have to change your grip and use the technique demonstrated here to take the back.

1 Royler and Megaton are locked in a standing battle. Both have collar and elbow grips on the other, one hand pulling on the back of the neck and the other holding the forearm near the elbow. Royler tries to push Megaton's elbow up and slide under to take the back, but he can't because of Megaton's stiff grip on his neck.

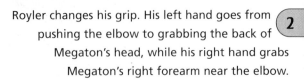

Royler changes his grip. His left hand goes from pushing the elbow to grabbing the back of Megaton's head, while his right hand grabs Megaton's right forearm near the elbow. **2**

3 We reverse angles here to better show the grip. Notice how Royler's right hand grips Megaton's forearm.

4) Continuing with the reverse angle: With a quick motion, pivoting off his feet, Royler twists his trunk to the right, throwing his left shoulder forward. At the same time, he pulls Megaton's right forearm forward and releases his head from Megaton's grip by circling it forward. Notice that Megaton will lose his base and lean forward, because he was asserting so much pressure on Royler's neck.

Royler quickly seizes the opportunity and steps around to take Megaton's back. From here he can use a variety of take-downs, such as the ones demonstrated in positions 5 and 6. (5)

6) Royler centers in base to control the back clinch or bear hug.

8

Between-the-legs takedown

Here Royler demonstrates another variation of a takedown starting from the standard grip. As in position 5, Royler is able to tap Megaton's elbow up, but rather than going to the back, he opts to use a crotch takedown. The back is your best option, but for that very reason the defender will try to prevent you from getting there. The between-the-legs technique is harder to master than takedowns from the back, and it may be harder to execute against a heavy opponent, but you get to this position quicker and can surprise the opponent with it.

1 Royler and Megaton are locked in a grip battle, each holding the other behind the neck. Megaton is applying pressure on Royler's neck, pulling it down.

Royler taps Megaton's right elbow with his left hand, but instead of going to the back he takes a big step forward with his left leg. Notice that Royler steps deep into Megaton. It is important to drop your hips very low for this takedown to be successful. 2

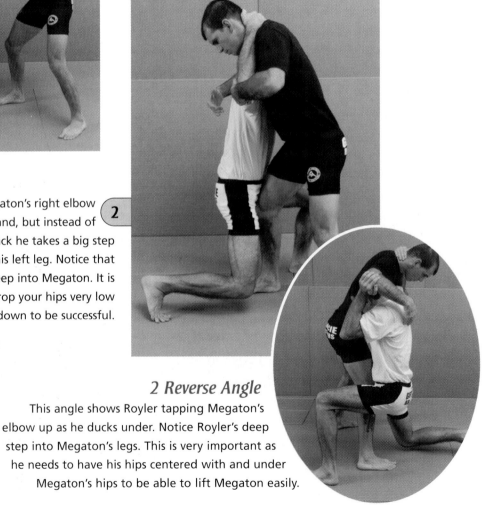

2 Reverse Angle

This angle shows Royler tapping Megaton's elbow up as he ducks under. Notice Royler's deep step into Megaton's legs. This is very important as he needs to have his hips centered with and under Megaton's hips to be able to lift Megaton easily.

3 Royler reaches between Megaton's legs from behind with his left arm and secures a grip on Megaton's right leg with his left hand, while his right hand remains in control of Megaton's neck. Note how Royler squats next to Megaton, feet square, torso upright, and hips pushing into the legs. This is the key to the throw: Royler must have his legs bent and square so he can lift his opponent straight up with his legs and not his back!

Springing off his legs, Royler lifts Megaton by the crotch while pulling his neck forward, causing him to be facing down. **4**

5 And drops him toward the mat.

Royler finishes by landing across-side. **6**

9

Single-leg takedown 1

One of Royler's favorite takedowns is the single-leg. He likes it because of its simplicity and efficiency, and because it can be applied from a variety of grips and positions (such as the double grip in position 10). Positions 9, 10, and 11 are all good examples of a key to submission grappling, which is thinking several moves ahead and disguising your intentions. In this case, Royler gets Megaton off-balance by pulling Megaton's head down as he goes for a snap-down. As Megaton reacts by pulling his head back, Royler moves in for the single-leg takedown.

1 Royler pulls Megaton's head down hard with both hands. He may be doing this to attempt a guillotine or a simple snap-down takedown. Note that Royler is pushing back off his right leg.

Megaton reacts by pulling his head back, yanking Royler forward. **2**

3) Royler quickly seizes the chance to shoot forward, arms open, to grab Megaton's right (front) leg.

Royler grabs behind Megaton's right knee with his right arm and uses his left hand to grab behind Megaton's right ankle. He completes the takedown by driving his right shoulder forward and down as he pulls up on Megaton's right ankle. (4

5) Royler continues to pull up on Megaton's ankle until Megaton is down on the mat. By retaining control of the leg with the same grip, Royler forces Megaton's back to remain on the mat. Remember that maintaining control and grip of the opponent at all times is one of the keys to attacking.

In this variation of the single-leg take-down, Royler has a solid double grip on Megaton's right arm. With this clear advantage of control, Royler starts off pulling Megaton down and again uses Megaton's reaction to assist in the takedown.

1 Royler has a double grip on Megaton's right wrist.

2 Since he is controlling the situation, Royler pulls Megaton down by the arm. Megaton tries to snap his arm out of the grip.

3 Using Megaton's reaction against him, Royler attacks Megaton's right leg, grabbing behind the knee with his right hand, driving his right shoulder forward onto the thigh, and pulling up on the ankle with his left hand.

Again Royler continues the motion until Megaton is down on the mat. Royler retains control of Megaton's ankle and leg. From here, he could go for a guard pass or even a submission hold. **4**

In this case, Royler has a single grip on each of Megaton's arms. Controlling the grip battle, Royler attempts to pull Megaton down. Again, the key to success is having your contingency plan in place. Royler takes advan-tage of Megaton's reaction and uses it to his benefit: Megaton pulls back and Royler releases his grip to keep Megaton off-balance as he shoots in for the double-leg takedown.

1 Royler has an outside grip on each of Megaton's wrists, clearly controlling the grip battle. Royler pulls Megaton down by the arms, with the intent of driving him to the mat, but Megaton defends by trying to snap his arms out of the grip as he pulls up with his torso.

2 Royler quickly releases the grip on Megaton's wrists, shoots in as he drops down, and attacks Megaton's legs, grabbing the left one just below the buttocks and the right one just above the knee. Notice that Royler has his head to the left side because of his grip (right hand higher than the left). Also notice how Royler is already preparing for the next step by quickly planting his left foot on the mat.

Royler stands up, lifting Megaton off the ground and over his right shoulder with his legs. **3**

Royler continues the throwing motion by twisting his body to his right (because his head was on the left side) as he heaves Megaton in the air. To enhance the twisting motion, Royler drives his right shoulder and head into Megaton. **4**

Royler drops Megaton on the mat, while still controlling his legs. Royler's arms are already in position for a guard pass. **5**

12

Hip throw to arm lock

Here is one of the applications of the warm-up drill in position 4. As he and Megaton are pummeling each other and attempting to control the middle, Royler gets slightly ahead and immediately goes for a hip throw, finishing off his downed opponent with an arm lock.

1 Royler and Megaton are locked in a positional battle.

2 As they exchange arm positions, Royler "swims" his right arm deep inside Megaton's left armpit, simultaneously trapping Megaton's right arm with his left armpit.

Royler quickly steps in with his right foot and turns his body in front of Megaton as he hooks **3** his right arm under Megaton's armpit, using it to lift Megaton for the hip throw. Notice that Royler is still controlling Megaton's right arm by grabbing it with his own left hand and trapping Megaton's hand with his armpit. Royler has his hips square and under Megaton's hips for the proper hip throw.

4 Royler executes the hip throw by extending his legs and throwing Megaton over his body, pulling Megaton's right arm across and driving his own right arm forward. Again, notice Royler still has Megaton's hand trapped with his armpit.

As he drops Megaton to the mat, Royler sets up the arm lock. Notice the grip Royler has on Megaton's right arm: the hand is trapped under Royler's armpit, the rest of the arm is grapevined by Royler's left arm, and Royler's forearm or hand is near the elbow joint. **5**

6 Royler places his right shinbone on Megaton's hips to keep him from escaping. Grabbing his own right wrist with his left hand and making sure his left forearm is behind Megaton's elbow, Royler places his right hand on Megaton's right shoulder to complete the lock. Royler drives his hips forward and arches his left shoulder back, applying pressure to Megaton's right elbow for the submission.

13

Single-leg trip throw

Another situation that can occur as a result of the warm-up drill in position 4 is the trip throw. As Royler and Megaton are in the over-under clinch, attempting to control the middle, Royler notices that Megaton's right arm is a little lazy. This may occur when an opponent is thinking about his next move or reacting to yours. Royler takes advantage of the relaxed grip and drops down to grab a leg and execute a trip takedown. Often, an opponent in this situation will hop on his foot as he tries to maintain balance, making the trip much easier. The trip work best when the weight is off the leg, although it can still work with the weight down. If your opponent is balanced or heavy enough that he doesn't need to hop to maintain balance, you'll need to switch to the takedown demonstrated in position 28.

1 Royler and Megaton are locked in a positional battle.

As they exchange arm positions, Royler feels Megaton relax his right arm grip a little and takes advantage of it by stepping in deep between Megaton's legs with his right leg and dropping down on his left knee, grabbing Megaton's right leg with his left arm. **2**

3 Royler steps in with his right leg and lifts Megaton's right leg with his arm. At this point, Megaton is off balance with his weight on his left foot, so Royler can continue to lift and try to take his balance away. Often an opponent in this situation will hop on his foot as he tries to maintain balance.

To better show the continuation, we reverse angles and can see Megaton hopping on his left foot to maintain his balance. Royler swings his right leg and drives his right foot to trip Megaton, simultaneously driving Megaton down to the right by continuing to lift his right leg. 4

5 Royler continues the throw, twisting Megaton to his right, and releases the hold, dropping him to the mat. Royler follows him and lands across-side.

Another option for a takedown from the over-under clinch is to try to take the back. Royler attempts that here, but Megaton's reaction—shifting his body weight to the right leg—prevents Royler from achieving his goal. Royler quickly switches to a spinning takedown.

1 Royler and Megaton are locked in an over-under clinch.

2 Royler slides his left hand to Megaton's right wrist. With his left hand he grabs Megaton's right arm just above the elbow.

Royler pivots off his left foot and uses his grip to pull Megaton's arm across his body, exposing Megaton's back. Megaton shifts his weight to his right to block Royler from taking his back. **3**

4 With his left hand, Royler reaches around the back and grabs Megaton's body just under the ribcage. Royler then begins to lower his body and pull Megaton down with him. Note that Royler uses his grip on Megaton's right elbow to help pull him to the ground.

Royler takes a big step back with his left leg and spins Megaton to the ground, pulling him by the waist. Note how Royler digs his fingers into Megaton's side, preferably gripping the hip or just below the floating ribs. This is a very powerful grip. **5**

6 Royler follows Megaton down, landing across-side.

Royler adjusts his position for proper control: he places his left arm behind Megaton's head and his right elbow close to Megaton's left hips. For additional control, Royler places his right knee close against Megaton's right hip, preventing Megaton from moving his hips and body, since his head is blocked as well. **7**

Considering the speed of submission grappling, it can be a great strategy when in the clinch to go for not just a takedown but a submission as well. Here, Royler and Megaton are in a clinch, and Royler changes his grip and goes for a Kimura hold. As he falls to the ground, applying pressure to Megaton's shoulder, Megaton can't help but follow him to the mat. There Royler will lock his legs to block Megaton's escape and submit him with pressure on the shoulder.

1 Royler and Megaton are clinched.

Royler moves his torso away and slides his left hand to Megaton's right wrist. He loops his right arm around Megaton's right arm. **2**

3 Royler starts to grapevine Megaton's right arm with his right one...

4 Until he locks his right wrist onto his own left wrist, making sure his arm traps Megaton's elbow.

Royler steps forward with his left leg and flexes it down as he sits, leaving his right leg hooked between Megaton's legs to keep him from stepping around. Royler sits down as he torques Megaton's arm up, forcing Megaton down with him. **5**

6 Once they hit the mat, Royler loops his left leg over Megaton's back to prevent him from rolling forward and escaping the pressure of the Kimura. Royler continues to apply pressure to Megaton's shoulder by torquing Megaton's arm around.

Side view of the submission: Notice that Royler not only trapped Megaton's rolling escape with his left leg over the back, but he also used his right leg over Megaton's right calf to prevent him from escaping in any direction. **7**

If you can clasp your hands behind your opponent's back while in the clinch, thereby controlling the inside position, you have another option for a takedown. By dropping his grip down around Megaton's waist and pulling this toward him, while driving his head forward on Megaton's chest, Royler forces Megaton to fall to the mat.

1 Royler and Megaton are in a clinch.

2 As the two fighters exchange grips, Royler gets ahead and wins control of the middle by having both arms inside Megaton's arms and locking hands behind Megaton's back. Notice that as soon as Royler has the controlling grip, he drops his body forward and raises his grip high under Megaton's armpits, making it difficult for Megaton to slide one of his hands back in and neutralize the grip.

3 Royler continues to drop quickly, moving his hold to Megaton's waist but keeping his head high on Megaton's chest.

4 Royler raises up, pulling Megaton's waist toward him as he drives his head and right shoulder as high as possible. By pushing forward on Megaton's chest, Royler forces him backward, causing him to lose his balance and fall.

Royler follows him to the ground and lands in the mounted position. **5**

6 Once in the mount, Royler adjusts himself, wrapping his legs inside of Megaton's leg and extending his arm forward for base.

17

Knee bar while in bear hug

You never want somebody to take your back in submission grappling—but if they do, there are counters. Here, Megaton has just put Royler in a bear hug. Once again, speed is of the essence: the time to spring this maneuver is while your opponent is still fighting for control and has not yet started any take-down attempt.

Megaton has Royler in a bear hug. Royler tries to break Megaton's grip by pushing down on Megaton's hands with his, but is not successful. However, Royler notices that one of Megaton's legs is forward between his legs.

1

2 Seizing the opportunity, Royler bends forward, plants his left hand on the mat for balance, and grabs behind Megaton's right heel with his right hand.

Keeping control of Megaton's heel, Royler does a forward roll. At the same time, he hooks his own left heel on Megaton's buttocks, forcing Megaton to roll forward with him.

3

3 Reverse Angle

From this angle we can see how Royler grabs behind Megaton's heel and uses his left leg to force Megaton forward as he begins his roll.

4 As they end up on the ground, with Megaton on the bottom, Royler still controls Megaton's right heel, now with his left hand as well, and figure-fours his legs around Megaton's right leg close to the knee. (Since he had his left leg between Megaton's legs, he uses his left shin behind the right knee on the figure-four.)

5 Royler applies the knee bar by wrapping his right arm around Megaton's heel and leaning back with his torso, pulling the leg back with both arms as he raises his hips, applying tremendous pressure to the knee joint.

18

Knee bar while in bear hug—supplex defense

In this variation on position 17, Megaton does not expose his leg to an attack and starts to do a supplex. In the supplex, Megaton would heave Royler over his shoulder like a sack of potatoes and fall behind him. Both fighters go down, but Royler would go head first. It is a nasty takedown that will often knock grapplers out if they land on the back of their heads. Royler's first concern is to defend the takedown by hooking his leg around Megaton's leg. After that, Royler goes for the submission.

Megaton has Royler in a bear hug. Royler can't break Megaton's grip, and can't attempt position 17 because Megaton's legs are back. On top of that, Megaton initiates a supplex.

1

2 Royler defends the supplex by hooking his right leg around Megaton's left leg, preventing Megaton from lifting Royler over his shoulder for the supplex. Royler takes advantage of the stalemate, looping his right arm around Megaton's head and grabbing his back. Megaton is no longer in control of Royler's back, as Royler's right arm is blocking him.

2 Reverse Angle
From this angle you can see that Royler's right arm keeps Megaton from returning to control Royler's back.

3 Once the position stabilizes and Megaton gives up on the supplex, Royler bends forward and grabs Megaton's left heel with his left hand. He can now safely release the right foot hook. With his right hand, Royler grabs the front of Megaton's right leg.

And rolls forward while still controlling both legs. **4**

5 As he lands on the mat, Royler does a figure-four around Megaton's left leg, close to the knee. (This time he uses his right shin behind his left knee, because Megaton's right leg was between the legs.) Notice how Royler pulls up on both legs, keeping Megaton from sitting forward and attempting any escape.

Royler applies a knee bar by grabbing Megaton's heel with both hands and leaning back with his torso, pulling the leg back as he raises his hips, applying tremendous pressure to the knee joint. **6**

19

Kimura while in bear hug

Another submission option that works when an opponent has your back is the Kimura. This is one of Royler's favorite techniques and mastering it will certainly yield you many submissions or—at the very least—reversals. This technique is difficult against a really strong opponent; in such a case, position 17 is a better option. No matter who your opponent, the trick is to use a sudden jolt to release the grip. It is important to note that Royler chooses to attack the arm that is being held by the other hand—in this case, the right arm. It is much more difficult to break the other grip.

Megaton bear hugs Royler, with his left hand grasping his right. 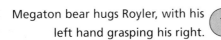 1

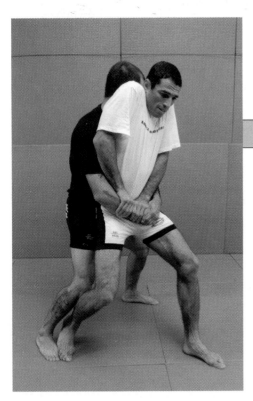

2 Royler notices the hands and decides to go for a Kimura lock to the right arm because the left is holding the right. Royler places both hands on Megaton's right wrist as he takes a small step back with his right leg, twists his body to his right, and bends his knees slightly. To use the best leverage, Royler locks his elbows in a frame and extends his legs, forcing Megaton's grip down, which causes a slight release of the grip and creates a small gap between Megaton's right arm and Royler's body.

Using that gap, Royler slips his right arm around Megaton's right arm, just behind the elbow, and locks his right hand on his left wrist. With that he has the necessary grip to proceed with the Kimura. But before he does that, at the same moment that he goes for the grip, he blocks Megaton's escape route by hooking his right foot behind Megaton's right knee, preventing Megaton from walking around to his own left and avoiding the pressure.

4 With everything secured, Royler breaks the grip by yanking it to his right, using the power of his body as he sits down on the mat and twists in a clockwise motion. Notice that Royler maintains his hook on Megaton's leg to prevent the escape.

As he gets to the mat, Royler further traps Megaton—preventing him from rolling forward or walking around—by looping his left leg over Megaton's right one and keeping the right hook above it, trapping the leg completely. By torquing Megaton's arm toward the mat, Royler applies great pressure to the shoulder. **5**

6 To add further pressure, Royler escapes his hips to his left and continues to twist Megaton's arm, forcing Megaton to submit.

20

Arm lock while neck is controlled

Although an opponent who has control of the back of your neck is in a good position, it is actually fairly easy to surprise him while he has his arm extended and catch him with this lock. On the down side, your opponent can escape this lock fairly easily by twisting his wrist, causing his elbow to point up and away from the pressure, but if you execute the lock in a sudden motion, it may yield a quick submission, as it causes a great deal of pain quickly. Once again, the keys are speed and absolute precision.

1) Royler and Megaton are standing up, with Megaton pulling Royler by the back of the neck. In the battle for position and control, Megaton extends his right arm slightly.

Royler immediately capitalizes on the opening and goes for the submission, trapping Megaton's right wrist by turning his head to the left. Royler quickly loops his right hand over to grab Megaton's right elbow with both hands just behind the joint, pulling it to his right.

2)

2 Reverse Angle

This photo shows the proper hand position for maximum pressure. Royler's left hand, already on the elbow, is almost covered by his right one as it grabs just slightly above the elbow, as close to the other as possible. This adds control to the arm as Royler pulls down and keeps the elbow locked, preventing Megaton from twisting his wrist to defend the lock.

Royler continues the pressure by pivoting off his toes as he pulls the elbow toward himself.

3

21

Double-leg takedown defense—sprawl

The double-leg takedown is one of the most common takedowns you will face in submission grappling. The attacker shoots forward, grabs your legs just below the hips, lifts you off the ground, and slams you to the mat. In addition to losing the points for a takedown and ending up in a vulnerable position, the dramatic nature of the throw usually pumps your opponent up, and the impact can knock the wind out of you. Here, Royler demonstrates the classic defense against the double-leg takedown, called the "sprawl." The key to the sprawl is to be able to shoot your hips forward and keep them pointing forward and down, with your legs straight back. If you bend at the waist, your opponent will be able to control your legs and a huge slam will probably follow. If you are late and end up being taken down by the double-leg, you must switch to the guillotine defenses shown in positions 22 and 23. On the other hand, if you anticipate the takedown early enough that your attacker never gets his arms around you, you can use the direct guillotine submission shown in position 24.

1) Royler and Megaton face each other, looking for a clinch opportunity or a takedown.

Megaton makes the move and lowers his body, preparing to spring forward and shoot in to Royler's legs. (2)

3 Megaton shoots and is able to wrap his arms around Royler's legs, but Royler immediately sprawls, shooting his feet back and pushing his hips forward.

4 Royler continues to push his hips toward the mat, keeping his body straight and legs back. The pressure of this stance will break Megaton's grip around the legs. Royler can then use his left hand to grab Megaton's right ankle and keep him from standing up and shooting in again. Additionally, by controlling the ankle, Royler may be able to pivot over Megaton and end up on his back. A guillotine, or a Kimura on the right arm, are other good options from here.

22

Double-leg takedown defense—guillotine

As in position 21, Megaton shoots in to secure a double-leg takedown, but this time Royler is late and falls from the take-down before he can sprawl. His next option is to go for the guillotine. He does that by quickly sliding his arms in front of Megaton's shoulders and wrapping them around Megaton's neck.

1 Megaton coils his body and shoots in. Royler sees the imminent attack but doesn't react quickly enough.

As Royler begins to fall, he places his arms in front of Megaton's shoulders and wraps them around Megaton's neck. Since Megaton's head is on the right side of Royler's body, Royler uses his right arm to wrap the neck. With his left hand, Royler grabs his own right hand, making sure the blade of his forearm is cinched tight against Megaton's neck. **2**

3 As Megaton continues with the takedown, Royler wraps his legs around Megaton's body, pulling closed guard. (Note that if your opponent has wrapped your legs too tightly, so you can't pull closed guard, you'll need to resort to the sweep strategy of position 23.) Royler applies the guillotine choke by stretching his legs, pushing Megaton's body away as he arches his back, and pulling up on his right forearm. It is extremely important to note the proper way to apply pressure against the neck; many people do it incorrectly and just lift their forearm against the chin, which is not effective. The proper way to apply the pressure is to pull your forearm into your opponent's Adam's apple, against the throat, as if you wanted to sever it. Hence the name "guillotine."

3 Detail

In this detail we can see the proper grip. Royler has his left hand gripping his right wrist. Notice how tight the grip is around Megaton's neck. It is important to cinch the grip around the neck before you apply the final pressure, otherwise you may tire and allow your opponent to escape. Since you already have him in the closed guard, take advantage of the control and adjust the grip first.

23

Double-leg takedown defense—guillotine with sweep

This position begins much like the previous one, only this time Megaton shoots in even faster and wraps Royler's legs tightly, preventing him from pulling closed guard. Unable to sink an effective guillotine from his position, Royler uses what is given to him: he hooks inside the legs, sweeps Megaton over the head, and finishes him with a neck crank.

Megaton coils his body and shoots in quickly.

1

2

Because he is slightly ahead of Royler's reaction, he is able to wrap his arms tightly around Royler's legs. Royler still manages to wrap Megaton's neck with a guillotine, but realizes that he can't pull closed guard as he did in position 22, and thus can't sink his arm with sufficient pressure to get a submission out of the guillotine.

Royler recognizes the new situation and quickly adjusts to it. He maintains the guillotine pressure around Megaton's neck and places his feet with hooks inside Megaton's legs. He will pressure the neck and use both the momentum of the takedown and Megaton's proper defense of the guillotine (he places his weight forward on Royler) to get the sweep.

3

3 Detail

In this detail you can see Royler's hooks inside Megaton's legs. The best place for the hooks is right behind the knees. Notice how Royler's toes point outward and up, really "hooking" the leg, which gives him more control and keeps Megaton from just jumping around them.

As he extends his legs, **4** Royler lifts and propels Megaton's body over him.

5 Landing almost mounted, Royler still has his hooks in and hasn't let go of the hold on Megaton's neck.

Royler releases the hooks, obtains **6** the mount, shifts his weight to his right by extending his right leg and stepping forward with his left foot (because he has Megaton's neck wrapped by his right arm), and pulls Megaton's neck toward Royler's own right. Royler opts for the neck crank, rather than the choke, because he doesn't have the control over Megaton's hips necessary to stretch him and apply true guillotine pressure.

The very best defense against the double-leg takedown is to be thinking far enough ahead of your opponent that you stay out of range of the shoot. Then you can let the opponent's forward momentum drive him into your trap: guillotine!

1 Megaton coils his body and prepares to shoot in.

2 This time Royler sees it and steps back with his right leg, moving his hips out of Megaton's range. Simultaneously, Royler shoots his arms straight and blocks Megaton's shoulders. Megaton still struggles to come forward and connect with Royler's leg for the takedown.

3 Royler takes advantage of Megaton's momentum, grabs behind Megaton's head with his left hand, and pulls his opponent forward and down.

Royler wraps his right arm around **4** Megaton's neck and locks the guillotine grip. He puts his chest on top of Megaton's head and applies the guillotine, pressing down with his weight on Megaton's back for added choking pressure.

4 Reverse Angle
This view shows Royler's arm position, forearm parallel to the ground and the blade of his arm pressing against Megaton's neck. The pressure is applied by lifting his forearm straight up.

25

Arm lock from standing clinch (arm is bent)

Royler's submission grappling game is extremely varied, sometimes using slow and methodical adjustments, sometimes using quick bursts to end things. His ability to change speeds and quickly recognize opportunities has translated into terrific success in competition. Here is the kind of opportunistic technique that Royler likes. It develops from a very frequent situation: you and your opponent are fighting for control of the clinch. Your opponent has his left hand pushing your right shoulder and his right hand gripping your wrist. Learn this position well and you can achieve some awfully fast submissions. Note that if your opponent has his left arm fully extended, you'll have to use the variation shown in position 26.

1 Megaton has right-wrist control over Royler's left arm and uses his left hand to push Royler's right shoulder.

2 Royler quickly recognizes the opportunity and springs off his legs, circling his body counterclockwise and shooting his right arm up inside of Megaton's left arm, breaking the block.

Royler continues the circling motion with his right arm and wraps it around Megaton's left arm, just around the elbow. Royler grabs his own right wrist with his left hand, even if it is still in his opponent's control (as is the case here) and pulls his right arm up, forcing Megaton's elbow up and cranking Megaton's shoulder joint for the submission. 3

26

Arm lock from standing clinch (arm is straight)

In this variation of position 25, Royler again takes advantage of an opportunity that presents itself early in a match. He and Megaton are again fighting for control of the clinch, but this time Megaton's left arm is fully extended.

1 Megaton has right-wrist control over Royler's left arm. He uses his left hand to block Royler's right shoulder and extends his arm to push.

2 Royler quickly recognizes the opportunity and steps forward into Megaton, springing off his legs. He turns in and shoots his right arm up inside Megaton's left arm.

Since Megaton's left arm is extended, Royler must adjust, trapping Megaton's left wrist under his armpit. Royler continues the circling motion with his right arm and wraps it around Megaton's arm, just around the elbow. He grabs his own right wrist with his left hand, places his right leg in front of Megaton's body to prevent Megaton from stepping forward to relieve the pressure, and pulls his right arm forward and down, pressuring Megaton's elbow for the arm lock. 3

27

Arm lock from the neck grab

A very difficult situation occurs during the stand-up battle in submission grappling if your opponent grabs your throat with his hand and pushes forward, forcing your head and upper body back. If you don't have a quick counter, you may very well end up on the ground, as he will force you off balance and either trip you or shoot in and take you down with a single-leg takedown. Here, Royler demonstrates a defense and a counterattack that go hand-in-hand.

1 Royler and Megaton are in a stand-up battle and Megaton gets an advantage, placing his hand in front of Royler's neck.

2 While squeezing the neck is illegal in most submission grappling competition rules because it can crush the windpipe, Megaton can legally push forward on the neck, forcing Royler to give up his base. Royler quickly counters the pressure by leaning back and clearing the grip hand by circling his left arm out.

Megaton is leaning forward as Royler steps in with his right foot. Royler wraps his right arm around Megaton's neck and reaches down his back. With his left hand, Royler grabs Megaton's right elbow. **3**

3 Reverse Angle

This view shows the proper way for Royler to grip Megaton once he releases the pressure. His right arm is draped around Megaton's neck, grabbing the opposite shoulder, and his left hand controls Megaton's right arm just above the elbow. His left armpit traps Megaton's right hand, and his chest is glued to Megaton to take away any space. (Remember, attacks need closeness in submission grappling.)

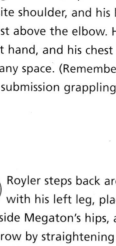

4 Royler steps back around with his left leg, places his hips inside Megaton's hips, and executes a hip throw by straightening his legs and pulling Megaton over his body by the neck and arm. Notice that despite not having the gi to grab, Royler is still very capable of executing the hip throw with simple small adjustments of the grip.

As he drops Megaton to the ground, Royler maintains control of Megaton's arm. To go for the submission, he puts his right knee on Megaton's right rib, making sure his hips are low and near the elbow, and he pushes his left hand down on Megaton's left shoulder to keep Megaton from spinning his torso and yanking his arm out of the grip. (Another alternative is to press the ground in front of the opponent's head or shoulder.) Royler steps around Megaton's head, planting his left foot in front of the head to block any escape.

5

6 Royler sits down on the mat, as close as possible to Megaton's right shoulder, and leans back as he applies the arm lock by thrusting his hips up, pressuring the elbow.

Once again, Royler and Megaton are in the over-under clinch and are fighting for control. Royler senses Megaton relax his right arm, and takes advantage of the moment. It is important for you not only to practice the positions but also to become sensitive to the subtle signals that announce opportunities. These signals may be a softness of the grip, a loss of balance, loss of concentration, an improper reaction to an attack, or even a counterattack. In this case, as in position 13, Royler reacts by dropping down and lifting Megaton's leg. This time, unlike position 13, Megaton maintains good balance and Royler can't force him to hop for the trip takedown. This is common if your opponent is taller or heavier than you, or if he is very flexible. So Royler must hook Megaton's standing leg and trip him for the takedown.

1 Royler and Megaton are clinched in the standard over-under clinch.

Royler senses a softness in Megaton's grip and capitalizes: He steps in with his right leg between Megaton's legs and grabs Megaton's right leg under the knee. **2**

3 Royler continues to step forward, now with his left leg, and lifts Megaton's right leg up, but this time Megaton is able to maintain his balance and has his weight firmly on his left foot.

Changing our angle by 90 degrees, we see that Royler steps farther forward with his left leg until he is square with Megaton, swings his right leg around, and hooks Megaton's left leg that was serving as a base, sweeping it off the mat. 4

5 Royler ends up on top of the downed Megaton. Notice Royler's right knee blocking Megaton's left leg, while his left arm traps Megaton's right leg. From this position, Royler has many options: he can go for a foot lock by sitting down with the right foot trapped, a knee bar by spinning around and over Megaton's extended leg, or he can pass the guard to his right through Megaton's legs or to his left around Megaton's leg.

Ground Techniques

Gustavo Aragao photo

If you are advanced enough to be practicing submission grappling, you should have already mastered the upa. However, this is such a crucial escape that it is best to give some attention to the finer points of the submission grappling version. The mounted position is one of the worst spots in which you can find yourself in any grappling sport. The opponent has great dominance over you and a variety of submission options. In jiu-jitsu, having the gi to hold on to makes your upa escape easier, but in submission grappling you must rely on proper grips and leverages. The most important thing you can do when mounted, of course, is not to panic. Many practitioners will try to escape in any fashion by just exploding in a series of misdirected bridges and bumps. This will only expend your energy and increase your sense of panic.

1 David is mounted on Royler. Royler starts off by keeping his head glued to the mat and his elbows close to his body to block David's knees from "climbing" to Royler's armpits, from which position Royler would have very little or no power to use his hips. Royler's hands are on his chest, ready to react and protect his neck from any attacks. His feet are planted on the ground and his legs are bent with the knees up.

Once you have the proper posture you can advance to the escape. In this case, David has his hands on the mat above Royler's head to maintain his position and his base. Royler's first step is to grab one of David's wrists, in this case his right wrist, with both hands.

2 Detail

Note the grip of the wrist with both hands. Royler uses the standard grip, with his fingers wrapped around one side and thumb around the other.

3 Royler pulls David's wrist to his chest. The power of two arms pulling one arm should be enough to win most of these battles, but if the opponent is very strong, you may have to wiggle your body up to the opponent's hand in order to gain control.

Royler controls David's right wrist with his right hand, keeping it glued to his chest. Keeping your elbows close to your body will give you the most power and leverage here. With his left hand, Royler grabs David's right triceps and uses his left foot to hook over and trap David's right foot. Now Royler has David's entire right side blocked and is ready to go for the upa. (Note that a wily opponent will sense this and try to free his hand before you get this far. If he is able to, you must switch to the escape shown in position 31.)

4 Detail A

Notice that Royler only traps David's right foot, not both feet. Additionally, Royler keeps his right heel tight against David's ankle to prevent David from slipping his left leg in and grapevining Royler's right foot to defend the upa.

4 Detail B

Notice that in this case Royler uses the "claw" grip, with all five fingers hooking on the same side.

Royler lifts his hips and bridges as high as possible. Once he reaches a high point, Royler pushes off his right leg and turns David over his left shoulder. It is extremely important not to try to turn to the side, but rather over the shoulder. To make the roll even more effective, Royler turns his head to the right and looks up, further clearing the path of the roll. (If the opponent foils your upa attempt by bracing against the roll, you immediately switch to the upa's sister escape, shown in position 32.)

Royler ends up inside David's closed guard. Royler's hands block David's biceps, preventing David from going for any type of control or choke.

In the previous technique, Royler demonstrated the standard upa, with the opponent leaning forward with his arms out for base. Here, the opponent is sitting back on Royler's hips, looking for an opening to attack.

Not only is this situation common in submission grappling, it also turns up a lot in street fighting, with the attacker getting ready to rain down punches. Whatever the scenario, the following defense works great.

1 David is mounted on Royler and is sitting back on his hips.

Royler closes his elbows tight against his body and raises his hips, bridging and pushing David forward. David has to brace his arms against the mat. **2**

3 With his hips still up, Royler braces his left arm and hand on David's right hip and circles his right arm around David's left arm. (Note that a wily opponent will sense this and try to free his hand before you get this far. If he is able to, you must switch to the escape shown in position 31.)

4 Royler lowers his hips slightly, but his stiff left arm keeps David's hip away from him. Royler traps David's left foot with his own right one, blocking David's left side.

Pushing off his left leg, Royler **5** begins to bridge over his shoulder to his right, making sure to keep his left arm pressing against David's hip for distance.

5 Reverse Angle

From here we can clearly see Royler's left arm on David's right hip, pushing him away. The left arm does two things: it helps push David over, but more important, it keeps David from thrusting his hips forward on Royler and taking away the power of the bridge.

6 Royler ends up inside David's closed guard. Royler's hands block David's biceps, preventing David from going for any type of control or choke.

A smart opponent knows that once one of his arms is wrapped while he is mounted on a foe, the upa is on the way, a move he will naturally try to prevent by pulling his arm out as soon as it is wrapped. Of course, if you have tight control over the arm, your opponent will have to yank his arm really hard and lean back to complete his release. Royler takes advantage of that in this little-known escape.

1 David is mounted on Royler. He is very tight and has his arms on the mat on the sides of Royler's head for base. David also has his hips low and tight.

Royler begins the escape the normal way, wrapping David's left arm with his right one and trapping David's left foot with his right foot. If David doesn't react, Royler will use the upa escape shown in position 29. **2**

3 Sensing the control and imminent escape, David quickly sits back and yanks his left arm out.

4 Royler bridges as high as he can, forcing David forward. David reacts by sitting back farther.

Royler quickly drops his hips down and sits up, twisting his body to his right as David drops back down. **5**

6 Royler continues his turning motion. He wraps his left arm around David's left leg, trapping it, pushes off his left foot, and swings his own right foot back through, sweeping David.

Royler lands inside David's guard with his hands on David's biceps. Notice Royler's position: he has shifted 90 degrees from the start. It is imperative that he sweeps perpendicular to David. He can't try to simply roll forward over David, because David's legs and feet will stop him. **7**

32

Upa variation—elbow escape

As effective as the upa is, it can still be blocked by an opponent who is able to free his right foot and brace against the roll. In such a case, you use the elbow escape. When used in conjunction, the upa and elbow escape become a formidable response to being mounted. If the opponent defends one move, the other will automatically be available. If the opponent is quick enough to defend the second option, you immediately go back to the first. This kind of exchange and variation is the key to success in submission grappling.

1 David is mounted on Royler. Royler has trapped David's right arm and foot and is ready for the upa.

2 As Royler begins to bridge, David slips his right foot out of the trap and opens his leg wide, blocking the roll.

Royler quickly drops his hips down, turning to his left and curling his left leg in. He brings his elbow and knee together, preventing David's leg from coming back into the mount, and slips his left knee just inside David's right thigh. **3**

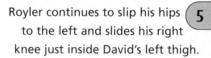 **4** Royler slides his hips to his left and wraps his left leg around David's right leg.

Royler continues to slip his hips to the left and slides his right knee just inside David's left thigh. **5**

5 Reverse Angle

Note how Royler's right leg is curled. His right elbow is blocking David's left knee, opening the way for Royler's right knee to slide in.

Royler slides his hips back to his right as he circles his right leg around David's left, placing him in the closed guard. **6**

33

Elbow escape to foot lock

Here is an escape from the mounted position with a twist. As Royler does an elbow escape, the opponent raises his body slightly to maintain position; this is enough space for Royler to go for a foot lock.

David is mounted on Royler. Royler has proper posture, his elbows close to his body to keep David from "climbing" up to his armpit.

1

2

Royler begins his escape with an upa, but David slips his right leg out and opens it wide for balance. Royler slides his hips to his right, uses his left elbow on David's extended leg to block it, and slides his left knee up inside David's right leg.

As Royler begins to move his hips to the left to continue the elbow escape, David shifts his weight slightly, raising his torso as he tries to maintain the mounted position. That gives Royler the space he needs to go for a foot lock. He pushes David's chest up with both hands, simultaneously planting his right foot on the mat. With his left leg, he lifts David up a little more and pulls David toward his head as well. This gives Royler enough space to loop his right leg under and around David's left leg, until his right foot pushes on David's left ribcage.

3

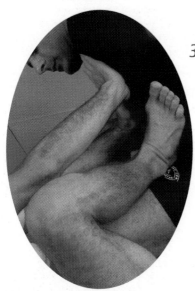

3 Reverse Angle

In this view, we can see how Royler uses both hands to push David away as he loops his right leg until the foot is against David's ribcage.

Royler uses his right leg to push David back, closes his right knee to trap David's left leg, and wraps his right arm around David's ankle. By locking his right hand around his left wrist, with his left hand on top of David's shin, he traps David's foot for the foot lock. Royler applies pressure by pushing with his right leg and arching his torso back, bending David's left foot back for the foot lock.

4 Reverse Angle

This reverse angle clearly shows Royler's right foot position on David's right rib. Notice how Royler closes his right knee to trap David's leg.

34

Escape from the mounted choke

So far we have not covered the situation where an opponent is choking you with both hands while mounted on you. Most submission grappling events do not allow the opponent to squeeze your neck by pressing his fingers into it, but they do allow him to push his hands down in a choking motion. This is enough for the person being choked to feel pressure and many times panic, giving up an arm or the back in a hasty attempt to escape. Here is the proper way to escape this situation.

1 David is mounted on Royler with both hands on his throat and is pushing forward for a choke. Royler's first step is to relieve the pressure on his neck. He hooks both hands inside David's wrists and pulls them outward and down as he brings his elbows close to his body.

2 With control of both wrists, Royler chooses a side for his escape. You want to go to the same side as the foot that you trap. In this case, Royler traps David's right foot, so he bridges over his own left shoulder.

3 As he lands inside David's close guard, Royler still maintains control of David's wrists.

4 Royler raises his torso as he pries David's hands from his neck and retains control over David's wrists. From there, Royler will posture and get ready to pass the guard.

35

Escape from the mounted forearm choke

A variation of the mounted choke—this one entirely legal—is for the person mounted on you to use his forearm on your throat. The opponent will cup his hand on your shoulder, put his forearm on your throat, and drive his elbow to the ground for the choke. As with the prior situation, this can apply a formidable pressure on your neck and create instant panic. It is important to master these upa variations, as each resolves a different and crucial situation. Note that all these escapes from the mounted position are dual-purpose techniques: they can be used as a series of good attacks when you are the one on top.

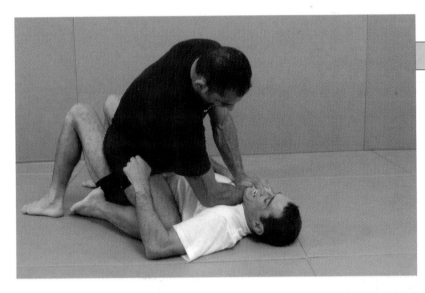

1 David is mounted on Royler, with his right forearm in front of Royler's chest. He cups his left hand on the back of Royler's right shoulder and presses his right elbow toward the ground as he uses his forearm to choke Royler.

Royler's first concern is to release the choking pressure. Royler grabs David's right triceps with his left hand and claws David's right elbow with his right hand. Royler brings his own right elbow down toward the mat, next to his body, pulling David's right elbow with his right hand. At the same time, he uses his left hand to help push David's arm in that direction, releasing the choking pressure. Royler traps David's right foot with his left foot and now has David's right side blocked. **2**

3 Royler bridges, pushing off both feet as he rolls over his left shoulder.

4 Royler lands inside David's closed guard, with his hands on David's biceps to control David's arms.

36

Upa escape—opponent controls your head

Many times, an opponent mounted on you will wrap his arm around your neck to control your head. By diminishing your ability to move your head, he achieves great control over you. Obviously, the best defense against this move is to have good posture and keep your head flat on the mat at all times. However, during the course of a submission grappling match and among the millisecond decisions and hundreds of reactions that you have to take, many times you will lift your head and give the opponent a shot at it. As a matter of fact, tightening the neck and curling up the head is a natural defensive reaction, and a common mistake that submission grapplers make. Here, Royler demonstrate a quick and effective way to escape using the upa.

1 David is mounted on Royler and has his right arm wrapped around Royler's head, controlling it. Notice how close David is to Royler, making it very difficult for Royler to move and find any space for an escape.

Since David's right arm is under Royler's head, Royler knows that the best option is the upa. He traps David's right foot with his left foot and grabs David's right biceps with his left hand, locking it in place. Royler also places his right hand on David's left ribcage and will use it for more leverage in step 3. **2**

3 Since David is using his right arm to control Royler's head, he keeps his head on the opposite side. This is a clue as to which side you should escape to. Royler bridges up and rolls over his left shoulder, pushing David's ribcage with his right hand as well.

3 Reverse Angle
This view shows Royler's right hand pushing against David's hips to help push David over and keep him from driving his hips forward, which would take away the power of Royler's bridge.

4 Royler lands inside David's closed guard, with both hands on David's biceps.

37

Kneeling guard pass

It is a fact of life that you will spend most of your time in submission grappling either passing or defending the guard, so you must master at least a few of those techniques if you are to have any measure of success in the sport. As was pointed out in the introduction, one of the most important factors in passing the guard is to maintain close contact with your opponent (except for some standing guard passes). Kneeling guard passes are particularly important to master because many times you will be fighting larger opponents. You won't be able to stand up and lift them, or even if you can stand up, they will be constantly forcing you off balance and back down. While there are a multitude of tricks to passing the guard, we are only going to touch on the most important ones, but examine the pictures closely and get further tips and details from them.

1 Royler is inside David's closed guard. David has his hands on Royler's wrists and may be pulling the wrists out to force Royler off balance. The first thing Royler must do is to find proper posture and not rely too much on his hands for balance to keep from falling forward. He does that by keeping his back straight and head up.

2 Once he firms up his base, Royler swings his torso to his left, takes a step out with his left leg, lifts his left knee, and twists his body back to his left, creating space between David's legs. Notice that Royler's hips are still low, keeping his weight back so that he doesn't lose his balance forward. Royler's step is out and not forward, to keep David from grabbing his foot.

3 Royler moves his buttocks back, lowers his torso, and braces his right elbow inside David's legs in the space created when he stepped out. Royler puts his weight on his forearm, pushing the elbow down to prevent David from pulling it back in and catching Royler in a triangle. At the same time, Royler slips his left arm around David's right leg, hooking David's thigh with his hand. (Note that if your opponent anticipates your move and manages to scoot his hips away, you'll need to switch to the pass in position 38.)

4 Pushing off his left leg, Royler drives his left arm and shoulder forward as he reaches to grab behind David's head with his left hand. Royler keeps control of David's right leg between his head and left arm and forces David's right knee toward his forehead. At the same time, Royler pulls himself forward with the help of his left hand, which is grabbing behind David's head. Notice the angle at which Royler pushes on David's leg: rather than parallel to the mat, which would just act like a plow to push David back, Royler pushes forward and up, deflecting any power that David can have and forcing his leg down. This is a very uncomfortable position for David and he will try to release the leg himself, yielding the guard pass. Notice that Royler drives his shoulder into the back of David's right knee, pushing it toward David's head. Royler also keeps his torso and hip close to David's leg for tightness.

Royler continues to move around David's leg and reaches across the side. Notice that Royler still holds David's head with his left arm and has his right arm controlling David's right leg to prevent him from sliding it in and pulling half-guard. **5**

6 Once across-side, Royler chooses to put his left elbow next to David's head, close to the left ear, to prevent David from moving his head. Royler's right hand is firmly planted on the mat next to David's right hip, preventing him from replacing the guard or half-guard.

In the previous position, Royler was inside David's closed guard and passed using the kneeling guard pass. This time, however, as Royler begins his pass and places his left hand inside to control David's leg, David reacts by scooting his hips away, creating distance and making it very difficult for Royler to raise David's leg. Royler needs to get David close before he can pass the guard, so he adjusts the technique to pull David in by the thigh, and then proceeds to pass.

1 Royler starts in David's closed guard. As before, he first gets proper posture and assures that he is in base, then starts to pass. Royler swings his torso to his left, takes a step out with his left leg, lifts his left knee, and twists his body back to his left, creating space between David's legs. Notice that Royler's hips are still low, keeping his weight back so he doesn't lose his balance forward.

Royler moves his buttocks back, lowers his torso, and braces his right elbow inside David's legs. Royler puts his weight on his forearm, pushing the elbow down. At the same time, he slips his left arm around David's right leg to execute the kneeling guard pass. This time, however, David reacts, scooting his body back and making his leg very heavy as he takes away the leverage that Royler needs to lift and pass. **2**

3 Royler must adjust and bring David close again. He grabs his left wrist with his right hand, making sure he has the top blade of his left forearm pressing against David's thigh, and lowers his buttocks until he is almost sitting on his right heel.

3 Detail

Notice the proper way to make the frame. Royler hold the top of his forearm, with the blade digging into David's thigh. His right hand grabs his left wrist, circling the thigh tightly. Royler's left shoulder is just under David's calf, close to the back of the knee, creating more leverage when he pulls the grip tight.

Pushing off his left leg, Royler rises up as he lifts David's hips and gets his own hips and body close to David. He pulls his left arm to his chest and drives his shoulder into David's thigh, pushing it toward the head. The pressure of the left forearm blade against David's thigh will cause a great deal of discomfort for David. Notice that Royler does not pull David to him, as that would be difficult against heavy opponents, but rather lifts David's hips and comes forward to meet them with his body.

5 Royler cinches the hold and walks around David's leg. Notice that Royler uses his shoulder to push David's right knee toward his head. Royler also keeps his torso and hip close to David's leg for tightness.

Royler continues to move around David's leg and reaches across-side. Notice that Royler still holds David's head with his left arm, while his right arm controls David's right leg to prevent him from sliding it in and pulling half-guard.

At some point, you will find yourself in a submission grappling match against an opponent who has a very active closed guard and constantly goes for submissions and sweeps. That makes it hard to use the kneeling guard passes, as you have to have perfect posture before you should begin that pass. In such a case, the standing guard pass is a better choice; by standing up you avoid a host of closed guard attacks. It would thus seem that the standing guard pass would always be the best option, but that is not the case. The pass also has its problems with base and stance against a player with good sweeps. Some people prefer the standing guard passes, while others are more comfortable with the kneeling passes. It is very important for you to master both and mix them into your game as needed. That being said, the standing guard pass presented here is among the safer ways to open and pass the guard. Use this when you are behind in the score and absolutely need to pass the guard before time runs out.

Royler is inside David's closed guard. David has been very active in breaking down Royler's posture and balance. Royler needs to pass and decides to use the standing guard pass.

Royler does a pendulum, swinging his upper body to one side, then the other. As he swings it to his left, he opens and raises his right leg and plants his right foot on the mat.

Royler swings his body to his right and does the same thing with his left leg. Notice how low Royler keeps his body and buttocks. This is very important for balance. He also keeps his knees close to his body, locking David's thighs and taking away his ability to move his hips and create a more dangerous situation for Royler.

Once he is sure of his balance, Royler extends his legs, lifting David's legs with him. Again, notice how Royler keeps his hips forward and knees closed and slightly bent. Having them bent allows him to react quickly, adjusting up and down if David tries to push up or down with his legs to sweep Royler. Having his knees closed prevents David from swinging his hips sideways for sweeps as well. Royler thrusts his hips forward so that, if David opens a leg, Royler can pass the guard by simply driving his knee forward and swinging his body around the leg.

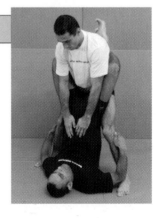

5 Once he feels sure of his base, Royler takes a small step back with his left leg as he lowers his hips and inserts his right elbow between David's legs, with his forearm pushing against David's left thigh. He also inserts his left hand in the space and wraps it around David's right thigh, grabbing David's right hip.

5 Detail Notice the proper way for Royler to grab the thigh. His right elbow is inside David's legs to avoid the triangle, with his right hand grabbing the top of David's thigh. His left arm is wrapped around David's thigh, with the hand grabbing the hip. This helps control and direct the thigh as Royler drives his left elbow up and shoulder forward and around the thigh for the pass.

Royler drives his left knee forward, right next to David's hip and in the direction of David's chest, as he pivots off his left foot, swinging his hips to his left and driving his left shoulder forward and around, deflecting David's thigh as he comes around the leg. Royler reaches wide with his left arm in front of David's left ear, his left hip touching the ground and right hand controlling David's right thigh as he lands across-side. **6**

7 Royler establishes across-side position, with his left elbow tight on the side of David's left ear and his right hand on the mat next to David's right hip.

40

Butterfly guard pass

The butterfly is a common and effective guard in submission grappling. With the hooks inside, your opponent not only protects his feet from possible foot locks, but also has many options for sweeps and arm drags to take your back. Ideally, the butterfly guard is performed sitting up, with your opponent pushing his head against your chest. Often in a match, however, your opponent will find himself with his hooks placed inside, but his back on the mat. This may occur as he is just placing the hooks or in a transition between moves. Regardless, as soon as it happens, don't wait for him to sit up; recognize the situation and use the following great guard pass.

1 Royler finds himself inside David's butterfly guard; however, David has his back on the mat. Royler quickly recognizes the opportunity and goes for the butterfly guard pass. He closes his knees, taking away some of the effectiveness of David's hooks, and places his hands on top of David's knees.

Royler pushes both knees to one side and puts his chest on top of David's upper leg.

2

3 Royler reaches forward with his right arm, grabbing behind David's neck. Notice that Royler still presses his chest on David's left (upper) leg, while also holding David's right shin with his left hand. This keeps David from being able to extend his legs and make adjustments like scooting his hips away to replace the guard.

4 Royler "walks" around until he reaches across-side. Notice how Royler remains tight on David and still holds on to David's neck and legs.

41

Sitting guard pass

This is the more common way of applying the butterfly guard. The opponent has both hooks inside your legs and is sitting up to one side, with one of his arms between your body and arm. This is also known as the "sitting guard." From here, David can sweep Royler with his hooks or go for a variety of submissions. Royler demonstrates his favorite way of passing the sitting guard. The key to this technique is to spin the opponent on his buttocks, then push him back to the ground.

1 Royler is inside David's sitting guard. David has both hooks inside Royler's legs, his left hand is between Royler's right arm and body, and his right arm is back to help him move his hips to either side. Royler, for his part, has his weight back and his left hand on the ground to brace the sweep.

Because David has his left arm inside Royler's right one, Royler wraps his right arm around David's neck and, with his left one, reaches behind David's right leg and grabs the left one, dominating both legs with one arm. (Note that if David had both arms inside Royler's, Royler would use the pass demonstrated in position 42.)

2

2 Detail This clearly shows Royler's grip on David's left leg. Notice that Royler reaches all the way around and grabs the outside of the ankle, with his thumb pointing up. This way he can fully control the leg, pulling the legs together and keeping David from extending the leg and maintaining the hook.

Royler spins David around on his buttocks by pulling his legs and head in a clockwise direction (to David's left). The direction of the spin is determined by which arm is inside.

3

4 Royler brings David to his side, with his back on the mat.

42

Sitting guard pass (sitting straight up)

A common variation on the sitting guard shown in position 41 is for the defender to sit straight up, both arms inside the passer's arms and his head buried on the passer's chest. In this position, since he is controlling the center of the action, the defender can do a variety of things: he can go for the side sweep by letting go of one hand, he can roll back and lift his opponent off the mat with both hooks (because he has control over the attacker's torso as well), he can go to the back, and so on. Royler shows a great technique to escape this hold and even ends with a submission.

1 Royler is inside David's sitting guard with hooks. David has both arms wrapped around Royler's chest and his head is buried there. Royler places both hands on David's shoulders and pushes back to create some space.

Royler slips his right arm around David's head between the head and left arm. At the same time, Royler pushes David's right knee **2** in with his left hand.

2 Detail This reverse angle shows exactly where Royler's hand goes: around the head, between the head and the arm, and between the legs. By doing this, Royler not only controls the head but also can reach the right calf.

Royler reaches around with his right **3** hand until he grabs the outside of David's right calf. Royler used his left hand to push David's right knee to his right so he can reach it with his right hand.

4 Royler locks his left hand behind David's triceps.

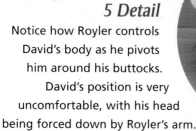

5 Detail

Notice how Royler controls David's body as he pivots him around his buttocks. David's position is very uncomfortable, with his head being forced down by Royler's arm.

5 Royler spins David around on his buttocks by standing up and pulling on the right leg and arm.

6 As he continues the spin, Royler slips his right knee on David's chest for a knee-on-stomach. At this point Royler has already trapped David's right arm with his left armpit as he wraps it with his left arm and prepares to go for the submission.

7 Royler lets go of David's right leg and closes the lock around David's arm with his left hand, grabbing his own right wrist and applying pressure to the elbow joint by thrusting his hips forward.

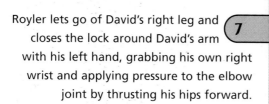

While very common in sport jiu-jitsu, the open guard is less effective in submission grappling because, without the gi to control his arms, the attacker is free to control your legs as he pleases. Despite that, you will encounter open guards quite frequently in submission grappling, because so many grapplers come from jiu-jitsu backgrounds and are accustomed to using the position. Therefore, you need to know how to deal with it properly. Here, Royler demonstrates a nice, quick way to pass the open guard. The key to this pass is to throw the opponent's legs out of the way and quickly step in with your knee. Quickness and cunning are very important for success, so you may want to feign throwing the legs to one side, then quickly reverse and pass to the other, as Royler does here. (In an actual match, you would skip step 3 or 4.) Practice the footwork in this drill several times on your own or with a willing partner, so that when the opportunity occurs you can take advantage of it. We start this position from the point where Royler has control of both legs.

1 Royler has control of David's legs in the open guard.

2 Royler grabs both ankles and throws them to his left as a ruse, making David react to block his own left side.

3 Royler then feints back to his right and has David blocking that side.

4 Finally, Royler steps in, with his right knee on David's ribs.

Royler puts his left hand on David's shoulder and his right one on the ground in front of David's hips. **5**

6 Royler drops down across-side, chest to chest. Notice that this time Royler is exhibiting a different arms position than in previous examples. He has his left arm around David's head, controlling it, his right elbow close to David's left hip, and his right knee on the ground close to David's right hip, blocking any movement. This is an optional position for the across-sides. They all work equally well; find one that you have the most comfort with.

For those who do not like to pass the guard standing up, a great option is to open the guard the traditional standing way and, once the opponent opens, shoot one knee through and pass down and tight. This presents a lot of advantages; it is a very stable and strong way to pass the guard that gives you options to pass to either side.

1 Royler is inside David's closed guard.

2 Royler swings his torso to his left and lifts and plants his right foot.

3 Royler swings his body to his right and repeats the motion, lifting his left foot and keeping his knees close to his body and his elbows tight to block David's legs and hips.

4 Royler extends his legs, lifting David's legs and hips off the mat.

5 Royler takes a step back with his left leg, places his right knee just behind David's buttocks, and drops down to the ground. That forces his knee in between David's legs and opens the guard. Notice Royler's posture: head up and straight with his torso, chest connected to his right thigh. A knowledgeable defender may block the knee with both hands to prevent the guard pass. If this happens, switch to the attack demonstrated in position 45.

(6) Royler shoots his right knee over David's left thigh until it touches the ground, making sure he keeps his toes on the ground hooking David's left thigh; otherwise David can close his legs in the half-guard. Simultaneously, Royler grabs David with his left arm under David's right one and his left hand around David's head as he locks his hands. At this point, it is very important for Royler to be controlling David's torso very tightly to keep David from moving his body and hips to replace the guard.

6 Detail Notice Royler's right toes still on the ground so his foot hooks David's left thigh.

Royler loops his left leg over and drops his hips to the ground, still maintaining the right hook over David's left thigh and the firm grip around David's neck and arm. (7)

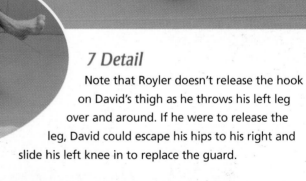

7 Detail
Note that Royler doesn't release the hook on David's thigh as he throws his left leg over and around. If he were to release the leg, David could escape his hips to his right and slide his left knee in to replace the guard.

Royler comes completely across-side for the pass. (8)

When faced with the potent standing guard pass demonstrated in position 44, savvy opponents will defend it by using their hands to block the knee from coming in. Once that happens, a great response is to simply slide your knee to the opposite side, deflecting the block. The mechanics of the pass are very similar: tightness and sliding your arm inside your opponent's arm are the keys. We pick up the technique with Royler already having opened David's guard using the techniques shown previously.

1 Royler extends his legs, lifting David's legs and hips off the mat. Royler's knees are together and his hips are forward.

2 Royler takes a step back with his left leg, places his right knee just behind David's buttocks, and drops down to the ground. That forces his knee in between David's legs and opens the guard. David defends the knee shoot by using both hands to block it. Royler simply deflects his knee entry to his left instead.

Still being blocked by David, Royler leans forward and slips his right arm inside David's left arm, under the armpit. **3**

4 Royler plants both hands on the mat for balance, making sure his right arm remains tight on David's armpit, and shoots his right knee over David's right thigh until it touches the ground. By keeping his toes hooked over David's right thigh, Royler ensures that David can't close his legs in a half-guard.

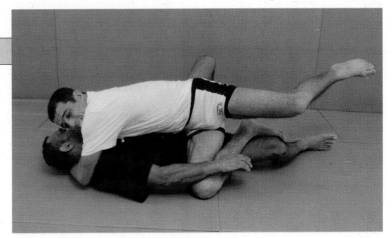

Royler grabs David's head and arm, wrapping his left arm around David's neck and locking hands. Notice how tight Royler's chest and head are on David. As Royler continues to press his body forward, he keeps thrusting his hips forward and driving his knee, forcing David to release the leg block, leaving Royler's left leg free. **5**

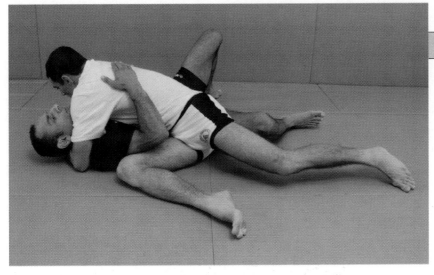

6 Royler slides his knee through, putting his right hip on the ground, his right leg forward with the thigh under David's right arm, and his left leg back to complete the guard pass. From here, Royler can go to any of the across-side positions he chooses.

Many times when you are passing the guard standing, your opponent, on the defensive and attempting a quick reversal, will open his legs and try a double-ankle leg sweep. The opponent opens his legs, lowers his hips to the ground, grabs both your ankles, and drives his legs forward and down, taking you down. In the standing guard pass technique (position 39) Royler addressed this, showing that you need to have your knees bent and be ready to "ride" the sweep by following the opponent's push up and down. Having bent knees allows you to react quickly as your opponent tries to

sweep you by pushing up or down with his legs. Sometimes, however, you will be slightly late and will begin to fall from the sweep, as in this position. All is not lost, though: as you are going down, you have a shot at a foot lock. You may also try this while riding the motion of the sweep. Once again, anticipation of the moves and their results is vital, because you need to position your arms and knees just right. If you are not mentally prepared for the possibilities, you will be too late. (If you react quickly enough, you can also fall forward and go for the foot lock shown in position 47.)

1 Royler stands inside David's closed guard and gets ready to open and attempt to pass.

Sensing his closed guard is about to be broken, David is proactive. He opens his legs, drops his hips to the mat, grabs Royler's ankles, and goes for a double-ankle leg sweep. **2**

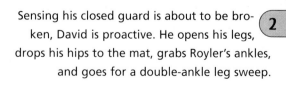

3 As Royler is being swept, he slides his right knee around David's left leg, placing it between David's legs, while closing his left armpit around David's right ankle.

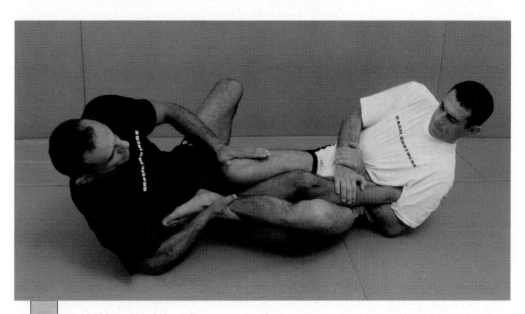

4 As Royler reaches the mat, he wraps his left arm around David's leg and grabs his right wrist with his left hand, locking the grip with his right hand on top of David's shin. He loops his left leg and places his left foot on David's right hip, leaning back to push David back. By arching his back and thrusting his hips forward, he bends David's right foot at the ankle for the foot lock. Notice that Royler's right knee is closed and between David's legs, which helps keep David from coming up and taking the pressure off the foot lock.

47

Standing guard pass to foot lock (falling forward)

Submission grappling is a game where the person with the most options and foresight usually wins. This position is a good example of the strategies and counterstrategies that often decide a match. As in position 46, Royler is passing the guard standing and David goes for a double-ankle leg sweep. This time, however, Royler defends it quickly by closing his knees, preventing David's legs from sliding down, which keeps his hips from reaching the mat. David counters by wrapping his left arm inside Royler's right leg to sweep Royler back. Royler defends the sweep by falling forward and immediately goes for a foot lock. This is a devastating foot lock, as the opponent gets trapped underneath with no real means of escape. Additionally, Royler can twist David's leg to his left and add a twisting knee lock to it. Royler employed a variation of this technique to win his first submission grappling title in the 1999 ADCC finals against "Soca" Carneiro.

1 Royler stands up inside David's closed guard. Sensing that his guard is about to be opened, David goes for the double-ankle leg sweep, grabbing both of Royler's legs.

2 Royler closes his knees, locking David's legs in place and preventing his hips from touching the mat.

2 Detail
In this detail we can clearly see Royler closing his knees, forcing David's knees together and locking the legs in place.

3 David slips his left arm inside and around Royler's right leg to sweep Royler back. Royler keeps his knees closed and leans forward (rather than falling back) to defend the sweep, until his left hand reaches the mat.

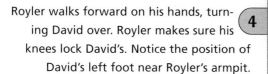

Royler walks forward on his hands, turning David over. Royler makes sure his knees lock David's. Notice the position of David's left foot near Royler's armpit. **4**

5 With David on his stomach, Royler braces his left hand and knee on the mat, locks his right arm around David's left ankle, and sits on top of David, leaving his right knee slightly off the mat.

Royler stands his torso upright, locks David's left ankle as he grabs his own left wrist with his right hand, and grabs David's leg with his left hand. Royler raises his right leg, placing his thigh just under David's calf, and arches his right shoulder and back for the ankle lock. **6**

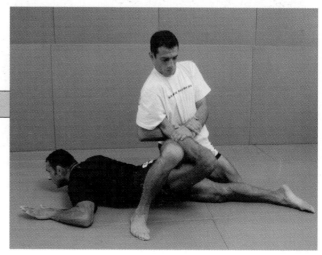

48

Closed guard sweep—foot lock defense

This technique is a good example of how to turn a defensive action into an attack. In this situation, David is inside Royler's closed guard and goes for the foot lock. Royler defends it by grabbing behind David's head. As David continues to struggle to secure the submission, Royler adjusts his body and climbs on top for the sweep and the mount. The keys to this technique are (1) to make sure you defend the foot lock, (2) to have a solid grip behind the head, and (3) to shoot your leg through your opponent's hold to relieve any pressure on your foot.

1 Royler has David inside his closed guard. David has managed to stand up in base.

2 Sensing that he is about to have his guard opened, Royler unlocks his feet. David starts to adjust himself for the foot lock, much as Royler did to him in technique 46.

Royler immediately defends the lock by **3** grabbing behind David's neck with his left hand, while thrusting his right leg forward so his ankle is well past David's left armpit. Royler controls David's left ankle with his right hand, preventing David from defending the foot lock by placing his left foot on Royler's right rib, which would keep Royler from coming forward. Notice that David falling to the mat actually pulls Royler on top of him.

4 David falls back, fighting to get the submission as Royler continues his defense. Royler's left hand still secures the back of David's neck, and his right hand controls David's left ankle. Royler climbs over David's left ankle and sits on that leg, preventing David from blocking Royler's escape route.

Still in control of David's neck, Royler continues to scoot his buttocks toward David, making sure he is on top of David's left leg, and slides his left knee over David's right knee. **5**

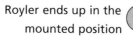

6 Pushing off his left foot and right hand, Royler thrusts his hips forward and reverses the position. Notice that Royler can't move directly over the top of David, as his leg is trapped, but rather pivots off the side, over his right leg. The movement is almost like circling around the knee.

Royler ends up in the mounted position **7**

In cases where your opponent has a very good open guard with great leg-work, and is preventing you from passing, you can sometimes achieve good success by going straight for a submission. The submission attempt has two objectives: if successful, of course, it ends the match, but even if it is not successful, it can intimidate your opponent, making him more con-servative with the use of his legs to defend the pass, as he now has to worry about the knee lock as well. Here, Royler prepares for the regular foot lock shown in position 46, but David is too far from him for perfect execution. That space between Royler and David, however, is a perfect highway to a knee lock.

1 Royler attempts to pass David's open guard. Royler always likes to have one knee between his opponent's legs for various reasons: blocking the thigh, setting up a possible foot lock, or just preventing the opponent from closing the guard again.

Royler traps David's left ankle **2** between his armpit, elbow, and thigh, preparing for the foot lock. His left knee pushes forward on David's right leg.

2 Detail

Notice how Royler traps David's calf between his arm and thigh by bringing his right elbow close to his body and closing his right knee in. This setup is used for both the foot and knee lock, allowing you to disguise your intentions.

3 Instead of going for the foot lock, Royler opts for a knee lock. As he turns his body to his right, he shoots his left knee through David's legs to the mat, sliding it over the hip. Royler pivots on his knee as it touches the mat, maintaining a firm hold on David's leg.

3 Reverse Angle
This perspective shows Royler sliding his left knee through the gap until it touches the mat. He uses this knee as his pivot point.

4 Royler figure-fours his legs around David's thigh, locking his right foot under his left knee, and arches back, taking David's ankle with him as he pushes his hips forward, applying pressure to the knee.

Open guard pass to heel hook

This is another great attack from the open guard. Royler has defended David's double-ankle sweep attempt and begins to pass the guard, but decides to surprise David and go for the immediate submission, applying the heel hook. Although the lock is called "heel hook," the pressure is actually a rotation on the knee, causing tremendous potential damage and tearing of the joint. For that reason be EXTREMELY careful when using this in training or practicing with a friend. This submission does not have gradual degrees of pain like most other joint locks; by the time the opponent feels pain, most likely some damage has occurred.

1 Royler stands between David's legs, with David holding both his ankles.

2 With his left hand, Royler pushes David's right knee out and places his own left knee in to prepare for the guard pass. Simultaneously, he pivots off his right foot and pushes his right knee in just around David's left thigh.

Royler wraps his right arm with the elbow around David's left ankle as he slides his left hand and grabs David's right ankle. Royler then falls back to the mat. **3**

Royler loops his right leg over David's leg and locks his heel on David's left hip, keeping David from rolling to his right to escape the heel hook. Royler makes sure his thigh is behind David's left knee. Notice Royler's right elbow locked around David's left ankle and his left hand holding David's right ankle, to prevent David from placing that foot on the ground or sitting forward.

4

5 Royler cups his right fist with his left hand and torques David's left heel for the heel hook.

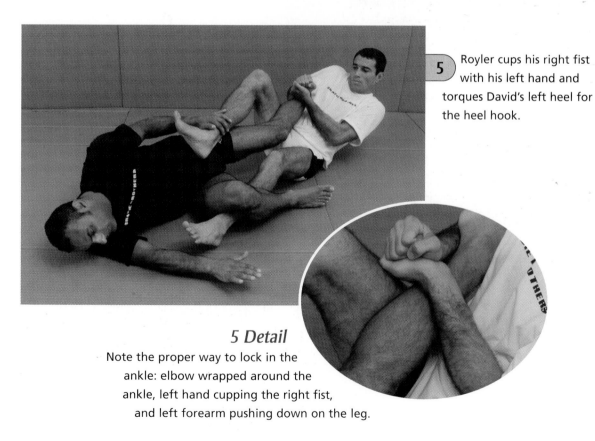

5 Detail
Note the proper way to lock in the ankle: elbow wrapped around the ankle, left hand cupping the right fist, and left forearm pushing down on the leg.

As in the previous two positions, you are attempting to pass the guard and may be having difficulty doing so. But in this situation, you are behind in points and time is running out. Consider a toehold. The toehold is a very quick submission when properly applied. The trick is to surprise the opponent and apply the torque vigorously from the start, as it can be defended with relative ease. In addition, you'll find that some fighters have such flexible feet and ankles that they are basically immune to this attack. And don't forget that, as previously stated, submissions always come with risk; any attacking motion you use gives the opponent an opening. In this case, if David successfully defends, he will have top position on Royler.

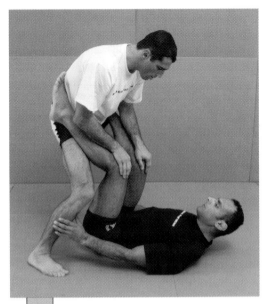

1 Royler stands inside David's open guard.

Royler starts as if he is passing the guard normally, his left hand pushing David's right knee down as he inserts his left knee to pass, and his right hand grabbing the outside of David's left foot. **2**

3 Royler quickly turns his body to his right and wraps his left arm around David's calf, while pressing his left knee on David's right thigh to prevent him from coming up.

3 Detail

Notice the grip on David's foot. Royler's hand grabs the outside blade of the foot toward the front, but not over the toes. Although grabbing near the toes would give you more leverage, it might also cause the grip to slip.

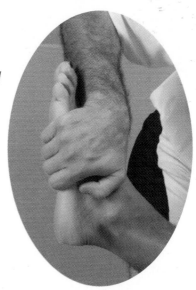

4 Royler pivots much like he did for the knee bar in position 49, his left knee sliding over David's left hip, with his foot hooking David's leg as he falls to the mat.

Royler closes the figure-four lock around David's left thigh, his right foot hooking under his own left knee. He completes the lock by grabbing his own right wrist with his left arm as it circles David's left ankle. He applies the pressure to the outside of David's foot, torquing it to his right for the submission. **5**

Passing the guard—foot lock counter

Never underestimate the element of surprise. In this situation, Royler is attempting to pass David's guard and is surprised by a foot-lock attempt from David. Royler imme- diately defends the foot lock by turning his foot in and counters with a toehold of his own. This is such an unexpected and unconventional counter that it has a high degree of success.

1 Royler attempts to pass David's guard, and David attacks his right foot with a foot lock.

Royler immediately spins his body to the right. By turning his toes in, he takes away the angle for David's foot lock. Simultaneously, Royler grabs David's left foot, with his right hand reaching over David's right leg while his left hand reaches under. This will lock David's leg.

2

3 Royler sets the toehold, his right hand grabbing the outside of David's foot and his left hand locking over his own right wrist. Notice that Royler's left arm, by wrapping around David's left leg and between Royler's own legs, traps David's leg as well.

3 Detail

Examine Royler's grip. His left arm is wrapped between his own legs and around David's left calf. His left hand is locked on his right wrist, while his right hand grabs the outside blade of David's left foot.

4 Royler rolls forward over his left shoulder and applies the toe-hold pressure by torquing David's foot toward the mat.

In submission grappling, having someone on your back is perhaps the worst position to find yourself in. The ability to escape this situation is immensely important; you should not only learn it, but master it by repeating it with a willing partner and then purposely placing yourself in this situation during training with better and better partners. Remember the three keys to escaping from the back. First and foremost, remain calm. Second, defend your neck with proper arm position. Third, recognize the correct side for the escape, and slide your hips to that side while keeping your weight on the opponent's leg to keep him from bringing you back to the center. The attacker's choking fingers always point in the direction of your escape—you always escape away from the choking elbow. Here, David uses his left arm to choke, so Royler needs to escape to his right.

1 David is on Royler's back, with many options of attack. Royler's first concern is to remain calm.

2 David starts to slide his left arm for a choke. Royler wraps his right arm around his head and uses his left hand to protect the gap on the right side of his neck, preventing David from sliding his right hand through the gap for a choke.

3 Royler moves his head to the right side of David's head, so David can't block Royler's escape with his head, and starts to slide his hips to the right, over the top of David's right knee. The hip movement is to the right and toward the top. It is very important to keep your weight on your hips to pin your opponent's leg down, otherwise he can just swing you back to the center.

4 Once Royler has his hips out and over David's legs, the choke danger is gone. Royler can now use his arms to brace David's left knee, which prevents David from rolling over the top and going for the mount.

Royler continues to turn to his right. He 5 will wrap his right leg around David while his left foot hooks inside David's right leg. Royler will then have David in his guard.

5 Detail
Notice how Royler places his hands: one on David's knee and the other just near it on David's thigh.

6 Royler slips his hip out and replaces his left leg as well, placing David in his closed guard.

54

Escaping the back—opponent puts foot down

This technique begins like the previous back escape, but as Royler gets his body to the side, David reacts by releasing his right hook and putting his foot down to help pull Royler back to the center. When faced with this move, Royler escapes by swinging his right leg over.

1 David has Royler's back. David attacks with his left arm, so Royler starts to escape to his right by wrapping his right arm around his head and blocking the access to his neck with his left hand.

Royler bridges, puts his body on top of David's, and begins to free his head to his right.

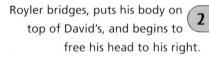

3 David sees that his choke is blocked and that Royler's escape is to the right. Sensing he is losing control, he releases his right hook from Royler's hip and places his right foot on the mat, pushing off with it to bring Royler back to the center. Royler feels the hook release and changes his escape: he grabs David's left wrist with his right hand, while his left hand grabs David's left biceps to keep David from wrapping the arm around Royler's neck for a choke.

3 Reverse Angle

Here we can see Royler's grip on David's arm, with his right hand controlling the wrist and his left controlling the biceps.

Without the hook in place, David can't stop Royler from kicking his right leg over to his left and rolling his body around David's left leg. Royler helps himself over by pulling on David's left arm as well. This is very important, as it keeps David from following around and taking the back again.

4

5 Royler continues moving around David's leg and pulling on his arm.

Royler lands on the side of David. **6**

55

Escaping the back—opponent locks his feet

Crossing the feet while on someone's back is a huge mistake, but in the heat of battle, even experienced fighters end up doing it. Be alert for the mistake, and if it happens, execute this foot lock for a quick submission. In this case, Royler actually creates the mistake by pulling and crossing David's feet.

1 David has Royler's back.

2 Royler raises his right arm to block a possible choke, grabs David's left foot with his left hand, and pulls the foot over David's right one, crossing them.

3 Royler keeps control over David's left foot with his left hand until he loops his left leg over the foot, locking his own foot under his right knee in a figure-four.

With David's foot solidly locked in place, Royler raises his hips, using both hands to push on David's right knee for the foot lock. Note that the pressure is actually on David's left ankle. 4

56

Escaping the back—opponent figure-fours the body

A common and extremely effective way to maintain back position is for the attacker to lock a figure-four around your waist. This is actually one of Royler's favorite controlling positions when he takes the back. The key to defending it is to spring the escape before the opponent can "hide" his foot behind your back. If you are late, then you have to somehow dig the foot out before you can begin to use this escape. Additionally, as is the case with all back defenses, make sure you protect your neck from the choke.

1 David takes Royler's back and begins to lock a figure-four frame around Royler's waist. He loops his right leg over Royler's waist and locks his left leg over his own right foot. His next move is to hook his left foot behind Royler's back or left knee to completely seal the lock. Royler first protects his neck from a possible choke with his right arm draped around his head and his left hand grabbing David's left arm.

Royler quickly switches grips, **2** replacing his left-hand grip on David's wrist with his right-hand one, and using his left hand to grab David's left foot.

3. Royler pulls David's foot over his left thigh and places it between his legs.

4. Royler loops his left leg over David's left foot, locking his own left foot under his own right knee. Royler then uses his hands to push on David's right knee.

5. Royler applies the final pressure by arching his torso back and to his left as he lifts his hips and pushes David's right knee with both hands. The pressure of Royler's hips pressing up against David's right leg causes pain to David's right knee and ankle.

Since you spend most of your time in submission grappling either defending or passing the guard, you naturally often end up in the transitional position that is the half-guard. These days, many fighters use the half-guard as an offensive position, with its own variety of sweeps and submissions, but traditionally and most commonly, the half-guard is a step between passing the guard or having your guard passed. In this position, Royler gets caught in David's half-guard and shows an excellent way to pass it. The key to this technique is to control your opponent's head and neck, with your arms wrapped under his armpit and around his head, and to keep his back flat on the mat. If, during the struggle, your opponent manages to slip his left arm back under your armpit, you need to readjust your position; otherwise, he is halfway to taking your back.

1 Royler is in David's half-guard. His left arm is under David's head, his right arm is near David's left hip, and his right leg is trapped between David's legs. David has proper position, with his left arm under Royler's right arm. To prepare for the pass, Royler moves his right foot as close as possible to David and positions his right knee up under David's left knee.

Royler needs to free his right knee. He starts by bracing his right forearm on David's thigh, blocking it. At the same time, he pushes off his toes, forcing his right knee through the gap. The frame formed by Royler's right forearm on David's leg will help prevent David from "climbing" his legs back over Royler's knee.

2

3 Royler leans back and slips his right arm under David's left one. If your opponent turns into you with his arm under your armpit, you should switch to the attack shown in position 59.

4 Royler locks his hands around David's arm and head, with his left shoulder pressing on David's chin. Notice Royler's right arm is up close to David's armpit so David can't easily replace the arm position.

Once he feels he has full control of David's head and neck, Royler **5** places all his weight on his chest, raises his hips, and shifts his right knee to the right side of David's hips.

5 Reverse Angle
Note how Royler pushes off his toes and slides his right knee to the right side of David's hips.

Continued on next page

6 Royler forces his right knee as far out as possible, until his right foot is the only thing still being controlled by David's legs.

6 Reverse Angle
This view shows Royler sliding his knee as far as possible, leaving only his right foot trapped by David's legs.

7 Royler places his left foot on David's left knee and pushes it back, releasing his own right foot and shooting it forward. At all times, Royler is tight on David's head and arm, almost suffocating him as he pushes his chest forward. This pressure is the key to the move, because David can't move his body if he is locked flat on the mat with his head and arm trapped.

7 Reverse Angle A

Note how Royler uses his left foot to push on David's left knee until he can slip his foot out.

7 Reverse Angle B

Royler pushes off his left foot and drives his hips and knee forward, making it impossible for David to keep the right foot trapped.

8 Royler brings his left leg back to the mat, and the guard is passed.

8 Reverse Angle

Note Royler's position, right leg forward and left foot on the mat, ready to adjust his body position if necessary.

Another good option when confronted with the half-guard is to pass directly to the mount. Many people prefer the previous technique of passing to side control, because of its stability and power, but the pass to the mount can be almost as stable as the previous one, and because it is less common, it will be unexpected. The key to this pass is to maintain stability and be prepared for a possible bridge or bump once you hit step 5, the riskiest part of the technique.

1 Royler is in David's half-guard and begins the move as in the previous technique, bracing his right forearm against David's left thigh and slipping his right knee out.

Royler slips his right arm under David's left one. **2**

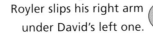

3 Royler cinches his arms around David's head and arm.

4 Rather than going for across-side position, Royler goes directly to the mount and drives his right knee toward the ground, placing his body on top of David. Royler's foot is still trapped.

Royler raises his hips, hooks his left foot inside David's right thigh, and uses it to open David's right knee up, forcing David to release Royler's left foot. At this point, Royler is at the most vulnerable part of the technique: his entire body is over David's body and his feet are tied up. He needs to be ready for David to release the lock, upa (bridge) to his right, and roll over. Should that happen, let go of everything, open your arms and legs, and brace to stop the roll.

5

5 Reverse Angle This view shows Royler's hips high, head forward, and left foot hooked inside David's right knee, forcing it out.

6 Royler obtains the mount.

Sometimes when you attempt the half-guard pass demonstrated in position 57, your opponent will hide his arm under your armpit, keeping you from getting inside his arm. In that case, it is better to use the jump-over technique, rather than fight for arm control. The resulting delay could give your opponent time to turn to all fours, replace the full guard, or even attempt to get to your back.

1 Royler braces his right elbow against David's left thigh and starts to work his right knee out of David's legs. David hides his left arm under Royler's right armpit and begins to turn into him.

1 Reverse Angle
Note Royler's body and leg position as he braces to release the knee. Also notice how David drives his left arm under Royler's armpit, preventing Royler from sliding his arm through.

2 Royler immediately changes tactics, wrapping his right arm around David's head.

Royler raises his hips, braces
off his left hand, and pushes
off his left foot.

3

Royler jumps to the opposite side
(his right), landing with his left
foot on the mat and keeping
his knee up for base.

4

Royler locks his right heel on
the mat, pulls on David's left
foot with both hands, and
arches his body back for the
calf lock. The pressure comes
from Royler's right shin pushing
against the back of David's
left calf. (If David's legs were
reversed, Royler would use
the attack demonstrated in
position 60 instead.)

5

5 Reverse Angle
From here we can see Royler locking his right heel on the mat and pulling David's
left foot back, forcing the calf against Royler's right shin.

This technique is similar to the previous one, but because David's feet are locked in reverse order, with his left leg over his right foot, Royler can't go for the calf-slicer. However, as Royler likes to say, "When one door closes, four windows open!" Since the left leg is over the right foot, there is nothing stopping it from being leg locked, and Royler seizes the opportunity.

1 Royler braces his right elbow against David's left thigh and starts to work his right knee out of David's legs. David hides his left arm under Royler's right armpit and begins to turn into him, so Royler immediately changes tactics and wraps his right arm around David's head.

Royler raises his hips, braces off his left hand, and pushes off his left foot.

2

3 Royler jumps to the opposite side (his right), landing with his left foot on the mat and keeping his knee up for base. Royler checks out David's leg position and sees that he can't use the calf lock on David's left leg, but that the left leg is now vulnerable to a leg lock.

3 Detail

This view shows David's foot position, left leg over right foot, which prevents the calf lock but opens up the knee bar.

Royler grabs David's left foot with both hands, **4** one hand on the back of the heel and the other just above it, for best leverage.

5 Royler, his right leg already between David's legs, closes a figure-four around David's left leg, locking his right foot his own left knee and pulling David's leg straight as he raises his hips for the knee bar.

Across-side arm lock

Royler believes that across-side is one of the most stable and secure positions in submission grappling. Therefore, he has developed a great number of submission techniques specifically for that position. Here, he demonstrates the arm lock to the near arm. This is a very sneaky and painful arm lock, so exercise caution when practicing it with your partner. The key is to disguise your intentions of getting the near arm by just locking it between your leg and elbow; if you were to grab the left elbow with your hand, your opponent would sense your intent and turn quickly to his right to release the elbow.

1 Royler is across-side on David, with both his arms to David's left side. David has a defensive posture, his hands under Royler's armpits.

2 Royler goes for the knee-on-stomach, his right knee on David's stomach. He traps David's right arm by keeping his own right elbow tight against his right thigh. Royler keeps his left hand and knee on the mat for balance.

3 Royler's left hand on the mat locks David's head and prevents David from turning or escaping his hips. Royler puts his left leg over David's head as he plants his foot on the outside and begins to sit back on the mat. Notice how David's arm is fully locked by Royler's arm, hip, and leg.

Royler sits back, applying the arm lock. Notice that since David's right wrist is trapped behind Royler's back, under the right armpit, and his elbow and arm are over Royler's hips, it will take very little arching to create the submission with pressure on the elbow. **4**

Royler favors foot locks in submission grappling because they are easy and quick to execute and the pain they deliver guarantees a high rate of success. As in the previous position, Royler starts with the knee-on-stomach and takes advantage of a gap created by David's leg position—right foot on top of the left knee, blocking Royler's mount—to slip in a foot lock.

1   Royler is across-side on David. David has his right foot on top of his left knee to prevent Royler from mounting him.

Royler springs up to knee-on-stomach, his right knee on David's stomach, his right hand pushing on David's left hip, and his left hand pushing down on David's throat to create a distraction.   **2**

3   As David fights to release the pressure on his throat, Royler moves his knee and puts it between the gap in David's legs, maintaining his right hand on David's hip while closing his right elbow, trapping David's right ankle.

3 Detail
Note the exact position of Royler's right knee in the gap in David's legs.

4 Royler drops to the mat, pulling David's right foot with him, and slips his right knee between David's legs to keep him from coming up to defend the lock. At the same time, Royler places his left foot on David's right hip to keep him away, locks a figure-four around David's ankle, and arches his torso back for the foot lock.

4 Detail
Note Royler's grip around David's ankle. Locking the figure-four right under the Achilles tendon produces the greatest leverage and pain.

4 Reverse Angle
From this view, we can see Royler's left foot on David's right hip to keep him away.

Another great option for a submission from across-side involves moving around to the north-south position. As you move to the opposite side, look for a submission opening such as an Americana or Kimura.

Royler is across-side on David, with both arms to the left of David's body. David's right arm is well defended under Royler's right hip and his left hand is against Royler's left hip.

1

2 Royler swings left to the north-south position and uses his right hand to stop David's right arm from following him around. He also leaves his right knee in front of David's head, blocking it. This is very important; otherwise, David can circle in a counterclockwise motion to defend the lock.

Royler wraps his left arm inside David's left arm and locks his left hand on his own right wrist as he steps forward with his left foot.

3

3 Reverse Angle

Note Royler's right knee blocking David's head and his hold on David's arm.

Pushing off his left foot, Royler torques David's arm to his right.

4

4 Reverse Angle

Notice that Royler first moves David's arm over to his right. Many times, David will be holding on to his shorts to prevent the lock, so Royler prevents this by raising the arm up. He also does this so that on the return motion he won't hit David's side with the arm.

5 Royler brings the arm back around to his left for the Americana or Kimura lock, applying pressure to the shoulder joint.

The arm is more difficult to submit in submission grappling than in jiu-jitsu, because the slippery opponent only needs to slide his elbow out of the grip to defend the attack. Because of that, Royler prefers high-control, multiple-option submissions when attacking the arm. By dominating the far arm *and* the near arm, Royler gives himself quite a few options for attack: he can go for a key lock on David's left arm, a straight arm lock by pressing the elbow during step 3, or the arm lock that develops here, in which he fully controls the elbow and the opponent's escape route, with his right thigh blocking the right shoulder.

1 Royler is across-side on David.

2 Royler gives a little space, inducing David to turn to his right, lifting his right shoulder off the mat and exposing his right arm.

Royler wraps his right arm around David's left arm and holds the shoulder. At this point, Royler will attack that left elbow by pressing it against his chest with his forearm while locking the wrist with his head. This move has to be executed quickly and sharply, for it is relatively easy to defend. For this example, David escapes in time by turning his wrist.

3

3 Detail Notice how Royler turns his head to his right shoulder to prevent David from turning his wrist, as he presses David's elbow to his chest with his forearm.

4 Pushing off his left foot, Royler moves his right knee forward, switching his hips, and grabs under David's right elbow with his left hand. Simultaneously, Royler locks in David's left arm by placing his head on top of his open right palm and pressing down on it. If David attempts to circle his left arm around Royler's head to remove the danger, he will open himself to a key lock.

5 Detail
Note how Royler's left palm cups David's right elbow as he locks David's wrist under his armpit. Pressure on the elbow joint is the goal here.

5 Royler continues to move his right knee forward, making sure he places his right thigh under David's arm to lock him as he pulls David's right elbow up and locks David's wrist under his left armpit.

6 Royler loops his left leg over David's head, placing his foot next to David's left ear, leans back with his left shoulder, and arches his hips forward, pressuring the elbow.

65

Across-side to the S mount

If you are in the across-side position and your opponent has a very good defense, you may need to change position to launch a new series of attacks or to score more points to win the match. Here, Royler demon- strates a great transition from across-side to the mount. Many times, this surprising move stuns the opponent and gives you further opportunities to attack. The beauty of this move is its simplicity; you just float over the opponent with your leg.

1 Royler is across- side on David.

2 Pushing off his left foot and bracing off his hands, Royler swings his right leg forward as if he is changing his hip position.

3 Royler continues circling his right leg over David, his right hip barely touching David's body. Notice how Royler balances off his left foot and right arm to make his body float in the air.

Royler continues his motion. As his right leg is completely over David's shoulder, he closes his left knee near David's right shoulder and puts his weight back on top of David. **4**

5 Royler finishes the motion, landing in the mount. Many times when executing the S mount, you end up with your knee trapping the opponent's arm. Although that is not considered an official mounted position, and will not yield points under most rules, it is still quite an advantageous position. Since the opponent will have only his right arm inside your legs, you can go straight to a triangle by pulling your opponent over as you roll to your back.

66

Across-side to far arm lock via knee-on-stomach

Usually, when looking for a submission, you have to induce your opponent to react to a move to give you an opening. If you just lie there across-side, your opponent will do the same and wait for your move to try to escape. In this case, David has his left arm in a bad position, in front of Royler's chest, with his hand between Royler's arm and head. This happens quite frequently in a match, and it is important that you recognize these opportunities. Form here, Royler can wrap David's arm and go for the standard arm lock by walking around David's head, he can go for the key lock by holding David's left wrist with his left hand and doing a figure-four, or he can go for this short arm lock by feigning the knee-on-stomach.

1 Royler is across-side on David.

Royler slides his right knee over David's stomach. David reacts by lifting his left arm slightly. Royler uses this opportunity to slide his right forearm under David's elbow. **2**

3 Pushing off his left arm, Royler raises his torso, after first turning his head toward his right shoulder to trap David's wrist, and drives his right forearm towards his chest, bringing pressure to David's left elbow. At this point, Royler's left knee is glued to David's right ear to keep him from turning to his right.

Royler places both hands on David's elbow and pulls it against his chest as he raises his body up. Royler keeps his chest slightly arched, because he needs to maintain space between his chest and David's arm. Notice that Royler keeps his head cocked to the right for control of David's wrist. **4**

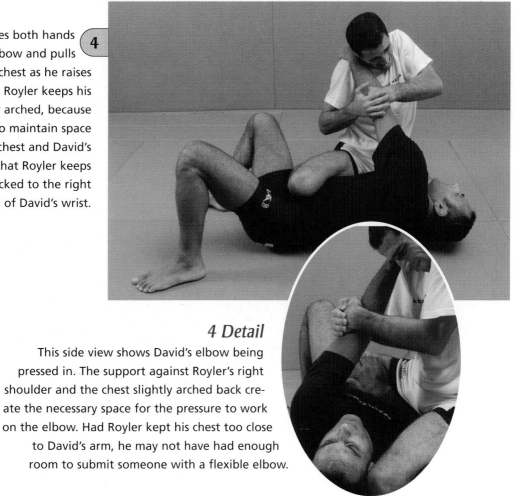

4 Detail

This side view shows David's elbow being pressed in. The support against Royler's right shoulder and the chest slightly arched back create the necessary space for the pressure to work on the elbow. Had Royler kept his chest too close to David's arm, he may not have had enough room to submit someone with a flexible elbow.

Royler loves this option for an attack from across-side because of its stability and because the lock is easy to apply and hard to escape. The key to this technique is that the opponent has to have a space between his elbow and his body for you to slip your arm through. This may happen during a scramble, or many times it occurs just as you are getting across-side and the opponent is adjusting his arm position. So be on the alert, and when you see the opening, go for it.

1 Royler is across-side on David and sees the space between David's left elbow and his body.

Royler slips his left arm around the gap and spreads his knees open for base.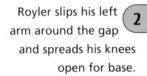

3 Royler locks his left hand on his right biceps and his right hand grabs his own left elbow, locking David's arm. At this point, as his arms are locked around David's left arm, Royler is most vulnerable for a bridge escape from David. Royler makes sure his knees are wide open and his hips are low to the ground.

3 Detail

Notice Royler's lock around David's arm. His left hand went under the arm and through the gap until it reached his own right triceps. His right arm goes around the outside of David's arm and locks on the outside of his own left elbow for a very tight hold.

Royler springs off his toes and slowly, keeping pressure with his chest on the lock, he walks around to David's head, with the arm still locked tight.

4

5 Royler shoots his right leg through, switching his hips, and cranks the lock by pressing his right shoulder down toward the mat as he lifts his left elbow, torquing David's shoulder.

68 Across-side—opponent grabs leg

This sequence demonstrates a common occurrence in submission grappling. You have reached across-side and control the opponent's arm for an arm lock or a Kimura. As you move to the north-south position or the opposite side to complete the submission, the opponent grabs your leg to keep you from getting there. Royler will take advantage of this moment and triangle the opponent's head and arm for an incredible controlling position. The control is so great that you can remain there for a long time and look for the opponent's arm until you get a submission—you can try the Kimura Royler uses here, or you could brace the arm between your head and shoulders and pull the elbow to you, as in position 66. Actually, most side-control locks will work from here, so be creative while your opponent is helpless in your leg triangle.

1 Royler has control of David's left arm and is moving from one side to the other. David grabs Royler's right leg with his right arm to keep Royler from getting to the other side.

Royler does a reverse triangle, weaving his right leg around David's right arm above the elbow and under David's head, locking his right foot behind his left knee. Notice that David's right arm was already grabbing Royler's leg, making it easy to lock the triangle. Once he has secured the lock around David's upper body, Royler grabs David's left wrist with his right hand. **2**

2 Detail

If necessary, Royler can encourage David into the triangle by pulling David's right arm up with his right hand and pushing David's head in with his left hand, but in most cases the lock will almost come out automatically. Royler also helps tighten the lock by pulling his right foot in with his left hand. Note that you must trap the opponent's elbow in the triangle, otherwise he can slip his arm out.

Royler locks his left arm around David's left arm, until his left hand grabs his own right wrist for a figure-four, and pulls David's arm up.

3

4 Royler torques his body to his left, taking David's arm with him and applying pressure to the shoulder joint for the Kimura.

69

Across-side to triangle

One of Royler's newest developments, this move adapts an old triangle set up from the guard to an across-side position. Again, this position will surprise most people, so don't use it too often and wait for the right moment to spring it. It helps to be very flexible in your hips and legs, so that the transition of sliding your leg through the gap will be effortless and can catch your opponent unaware; if you are not that flexible, you can improve your angle by sliding your hips up toward the opponent's head.

1 Royler is across-side on David with both hands on one side.

2 Royler reaches around David's head with his left arm, switches his hips—left hip to the mat—and grabs David's left wrist with his right hand. Notice Royler's right leg with the knee up for base. If you are not as flexible, push off your right foot to scoot your hip up, which will help set up the next step.

3 Royler opens David's left arm a little and slips his right leg through the gap between the arms and David's body.

4 Royler grabs his own right foot with his left hand.

Pushing off his left foot, Royler rolls forward (over David's left shoulder), pulling David with him as he opens his right leg to trap David's right arm. **5**

6 Royler lands with David locked into the triangle, David's right arm and head inside the frame. Royler locks his left leg over his right foot and can now release his left-hand grip on his right foot, since the triangle is completely locked.

7 Royler places both hands behind David's head and pulls it to him as he squeezes the triangle with his legs.

70

Across-side to forearm choke

Another great attack from across-side is the forearm choke. In this position, Royler starts out with his arms on David's left side, then changes his control position by wrapping his left arm around David's head. This is a very common controlling position from across-side, and David knows how to defend it: his arms are in the proper posture, his right hand controlling Royler's left hip and his right arm hidden under Royler's right armpit. Letting your opponent feel comfortable and out of danger is the key to this position, because that allows you to surprise him with a forearm choke.

1 Royler is across-side with both arms on David's right side.

Royler changes his control and wraps his left arm around David's head. **2**

3 Sensing that David is relaxed, Royler goes for the forearm choke. He locks his hands together, raises his chest up, and brings his right elbow toward his left one, driving his right forearm into David's throat.

Royler springs off his feet and brings both elbows together, choking David.

4

4 Detail
Note Royler's hand grip. Since his right forearm is the one on David's throat, his right palm faces up and his left one faces down.

71

Across-side to neck crank

Raising the head is a very common mistake when on the bottom. The opponent may bring it up when you pull a knee-on-stomach, when being mounted, or when caught across-side. A cagey fighter notices such lapses and responds decisively. In this case, from across-side, the neck crank can finish things quickly.

1 Royler is across-side on David, with both hands to David's right. David raises his head off the mat.

Seeing this, Royler wraps his right arm around David's neck as he slides his right leg across, turning his hips to his left. **2**

3 Royler sits on his right hip and grabs his own right wrist with his left hand.

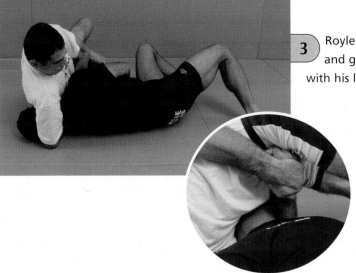

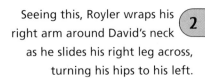

3 Detail
Notice Royler's grip, left hand gripping right wrist as his arm encircles David's neck.

4 Royler loops his left leg over David's body and lands his foot next to David's right hip, making sure he keeps his right leg flat on the mat, semi-extended, with his knee touching David's left hip.

Royler pushes off his left leg, places his head and right shoulder on the ground, and arches his body back as he digs his forearm into David's neck while cranking David's head at the same time.

5

72

Across-side arm lock to triangle

Often the progress to achieve an arm lock from across-side is slow and methodical, and a strong opponent will have time to lock his hands and resist. Rather than expending too much energy to achieve the arm lock, perhaps even losing the position, the smart practitioner can lure the opponent into attempting to escape by rolling over the top—only to fall into a triangle. We pick up the action after Royler has secured Megaton's right arm from across-side, moved around the head, and is in the finishing phase of the arm lock.

1　Royler has Megaton's right arm in an arm lock, but Megaton has locked his hands and defends fiercely.

2　Royler loops his right foot in front of Megaton's left elbow and eases the pressure on his left leg, which is over Megaton's head. The left leg controls Megaton's ability to free his head and roll to his right to get over the top of Royler.

3 Sensing an opening, Megaton slides his head from under Royler's leg, pushes off his left leg, and rolls over the top of Royler, thinking he has defended the arm lock. Royler allows Megaton to go to the top, as he wraps his right leg around Megaton's neck.

When his back touches the mat, Royler already has Megaton's head and right arm locked into the triangle. He pulls Megaton's right arm across his body with both hands to cinch the choke.

4

5 Royler places both hands on the back of Megaton's head and pulls it forward, while squeezing his knees for the submission.

73

Mounted key-lock to arm-lock combo

The more attacks you can coordinate, the better the chances of one getting through. As was discussed in the introduction, the key to the success of a multiple attack is to go for each attack with the real intent of submitting your opponent, but to be prepared for the defense and have your next attack ready to go. If you go halfheartedly for the first attempt, a smart opponent will not have to commit and will still be in position for your second one.

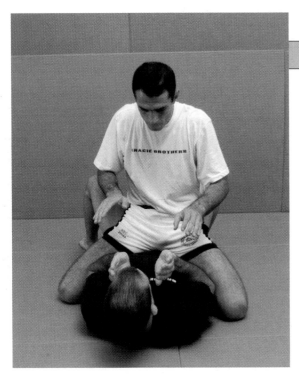

1 Royler is mounted on Megaton. Megaton has good posture, with his elbows close to his body, preventing Royler from climbing up on the mount. Megaton's arms are in front of his neck, protecting against a choke.

2 Royler chooses to attack Megaton's right arm with a key lock. He drives his right hand into Megaton's right wrist, his left hand pushing the elbow, and presses the arm down to the mat.

3 Megaton reacts to the key lock attempt by turning to his right and holding his right wrist with his left hand, pulling it back off the mat. (Another option for Megaton here would have been to bring his arms low and in, in which case Royler would have to change to the naked choke demonstrated in position 75.)

Royler quickly pivots his hips to his right (toward Megaton's head), circling his right leg over Megaton's head, and secures a grip on Megaton's left arm.

4

5 Royler stretches Megaton's arm for the submission. Notice Royler's feet are on the ground and his leg position is perfect—his right leg blocking Megaton's head—as he raises his hips, pressuring the elbow. Royler has Megaton's wrist tight against his chest; any space there would translate into less pressure to the elbow and a better chance of Megaton spinning his wrist and turning his elbow for an escape.

As previously addressed, multiple attacks are extremely important. This is especially true in the mounted position because the defender closes himself up to attacks, so multiple attacks can be the best way to get the defender out of his "shell." Here, Royler demonstrates a couple of options that he really likes.

He starts with the front choke and uses the panic this often produces in the opponent to slide into a head-and-arm choke. The key to that choke is to press the neck with your shoulder and his arm as you push forward into his head and close your grip around his head and arm.

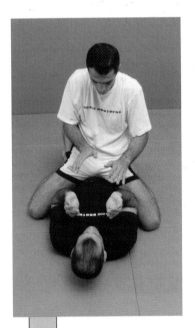

1 Royler is mounted on Megaton.

2 Royler goes for the front choke by pressing his open right hand into Megaton's throat, shifting his weight slightly to his right and pulling up on Megaton's right elbow with his left hand.

3 Royler continues to press forward with his body as he pulls Megaton's right arm across. Megaton defends the choke with his left hand, focusing on pulling Royler's right hand off his throat.

4 Megaton pulls Royler's right arm out, releasing the pressure on his throat, but Royler immediately circles that arm around Megaton's head. Royler traps Megaton's right arm with his own head and grabs his own right wrist with his left hand, locking the head-and-arm grip on Megaton.

Royler leans forward, putting his weight on Megaton's right shoulder and head, and jumps to his left (since he has his right arm near Megaton's neck). **5**

6 Royler lands on his feet and presses forward off his toes, already applying a lot of choking pressure.

Royler finishes the choke by lowering his hips and pushing off his left toes, pressing Megaton's right arm against the neck as he cinches the lock. **7**

Mounted key lock to front naked choke

Different opponents react differently to the same attacks. Here, faced with the key lock demonstrated in position 73, Megaton defends this time by bringing his arms low and in. This prevents Royler from using the technique presented in position 73, but he has another trick up his sleeve and goes for the front version of the naked choke.

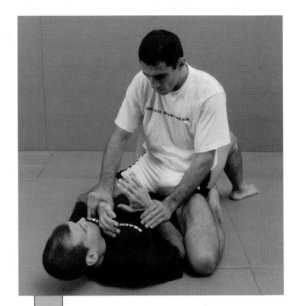

1 Royler is mounted on Megaton and attempts to control his wrist for a key lock. Megaton closes his arms in and lowers his right forearm, taking away Royler's leverage.

2 Royler opens his arms wide and lowers his chest on top of Megaton's arms, trapping them.

Royler wraps his right arm around Megaton's head and grabs his own left biceps with his right hand.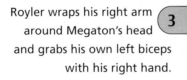

4 Royler closes the choke by sliding his left hand in front of Megaton's throat as he lowers his head. Royler makes sure he uses the lower blade of his left hand to press against Megaton's throat. If he used the wide part, he'd lose a lot of pressure.

Royler stretches his body as he **5** grapevines his legs around Megaton's, locking Megaton in. He applies the choking pressure with his chest pressing down and his forearms closing in, as he presses his left hand down on Megaton's throat.

5 Reverse Angle

This angle clearly shows Royler's left hand position, the blade pressing against Megaton's throat, and his legs grapevined around Megaton's legs to keep him from bridging to escape.

When you mount your opponent, he will often close himself up by crossing his arms in front of his neck. This not only protects the neck from chokes, but also hinders key locks and arm locks. Royler takes advantage of a seemingly difficult nut to crack and changes everything as he takes the back and applies a rear naked choke (mata-leão).

1 Royler is mounted on Megaton, who crosses his arms in front of his chest with his hands protecting his neck. Since Megaton is not blocking Royler's knees, Royler climbs up further, raising Megaton's elbows. (Note that if your opponent manages to keep his elbows so low and tight that you can't get your knees under, you'll need to switch to the attack demonstrated in position 77.)

Royler drives **2** Megaton's right elbow across with his left hand and helps the motion by pushing Megaton's right wrist with his right hand.

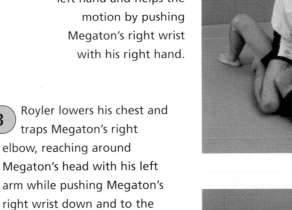

3 Royler lowers his chest and traps Megaton's right elbow, reaching around Megaton's head with his left arm while pushing Megaton's right wrist down and to the left with his right hand.

Royler exchanges his right-hand grip on Megaton's **4** wrist for a left-hand one and slips his right hand through the gap near the wrists. At this point, Royler has complete control of Megaton's torso.

(5) Royler shifts his body to his left, slides his left knee forward, pulls Megaton's head over his thigh, and sits on his left heel.

(6) Royler lies back to his right, pulling Megaton with him. The right foot automatically hooks Megaton's right hip. As he gets Megaton on top of him, Royler exchanges his grip on Megaton's wrist and slides his left arm around Megaton's neck.

6 Reverse Angle

Note Royler's handwork: his left hand releases Megaton's right wrist and is replaced by his right hand. His left hand wraps around Megaton's neck. Royler must maintain control of Megaton's right wrist until Royler's left arm is completely around Megaton's neck; otherwise, Megaton would have his hand free to block Royler's arm from going around.

(7) Continuing with the reverse angle, we see Royler lock the left hook, grab his right biceps with his left hand, bend his right forearm, put his right hand behind Megaton's head, and press the choke by squeezing his elbows together as he pulls his left arm tight around Megaton's neck. Notice that Royler has his head close, with his left cheek behind his right hand, for two reasons: it helps press the choke, and it makes it harder for Megaton to reach over with his hands and pry Royler's right hand from behind his head.

Mounted head-and-arm choke

As in position 76, the opponent has his hands crossed in front of his neck and his elbows are low, making it difficult to use a key lock or attack the neck with a choke. You can try to take the back, as in position 76, but if the opponent manages to keep his elbows so low and tight that you can't get your knee in (common if your adversary has long arms), then you need another solution. Here, Royler appraises the situation and decides to go for the head-and-arm choke.

1 Royler is mounted on Megaton, but Megaton has his elbows tight and low. Royler appraises the situation and sees that Megaton's right arm is over his left arm, making his right elbow slightly higher than the left.

Royler drops his chest down and his hips back, opens his arms wide, planting his hands on the mat, and props his left shoulder just under Megaton's right elbow. **2**

2 Detail
Note how Royler lowers his shoulder below Megaton's elbow to be able to get under it and lift it.

3 With his hands firmly planted on the mat for leverage, Royler moves his body forward and drives his left shoulder to his right, pushing Megaton's right arm across his face.

4 Royler grabs Megaton's right wrist with his own right hand and uses his head to lock Megaton's arm in place.

5 Royler releases Megaton's wrist and wraps his right arm around Megaton's head until he can grab his right wrist with his left hand. Now Royler has Megaton trapped in the head-and-arm triangle, with his right arm and head locking Megaton's right arm and head.

Royler jumps to his left and pushes forward **6** off his toes, driving Megaton's right arm in as he tightens his arm grip for the choke. Notice how Royler uses his head to add pressure to the choke as he drives his right shoulder down to cinch the lock and pulls his right forearm in for the choke. It is vital to make sure that the direction of the pressure is not straight up, but rather into the opponent's Adam's apple.

Because the across-side position is very stable for the attacker and is the launching point for so many attacks, being able to escape from it and reverse the situation is paramount for a serious submission grappling fighter. This escape-and-reverse technique works best before the adversary passes your guard and secures the position, but will work even if he is already stabilized across-side. The key is to maintain the pressure on the upper shoulder as you turn, which is accomplished by only changing your feet position once you have at least one foot able to apply forward pressure.

1 Megaton is across-side on Royler. Royler has good posture, his right arm blocking Megaton's left hip and his left arm under Megaton's armpit.

2 Pushing off his left foot, Royler bridges slightly to help escape his hips to the left. At the same time, Royler keeps pushing off his left foot and drives his left shoulder into Megaton, maintaining a brace there. This is very important; if you release that pressure, your opponent can just drive you back down.

3 Still bracing with his left leg, Royler steps through with his right leg and plants his right foot down to replace the pressure of his left shoulder against Megaton's chest. Royler loops his left leg over, turning onto his stomach, and reaches forward with his arms.

Royler continues his footwork, driving forward on Megaton until he is on his stomach and his arms surround Megaton's legs to prevent Megaton from circling to the back. Since he turned over to his right, Royler's head is on the outside of Megaton's right hip, so he steps forward with his left leg. Notice that Royler's toes are planted on the mat and he is pushing forward off both feet.

4

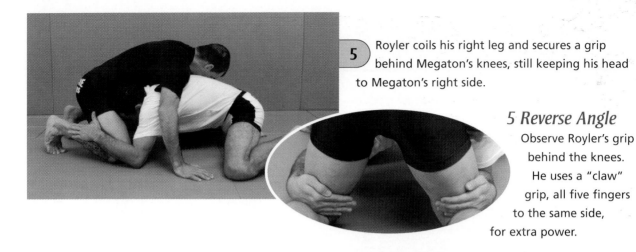

5 Royler coils his right leg and secures a grip behind Megaton's knees, still keeping his head to Megaton's right side.

5 Reverse Angle
Observe Royler's grip behind the knees. He uses a "claw" grip, all five fingers to the same side, for extra power.

Royler grabs Megaton's right leg just behind the knee by bringing his right arm between Megaton's legs, wedging his forearm behind the knee, and gripping his right wrist with his left hand to lock the grip.Notice that Royler's head is on the same side as the leg he controls.

6

7 Pushing off both legs, Royler drives Megaton back over his right leg, taking him down to the mat. It is important to drive forward to topple the opponent, rather than expecting to use your arms to pull him over.

Royler continues the move by standing up as he controls Megaton's right arm with his left hand and keeps his right arm around Megaton's right knee. Notice that Royler has Megaton's right leg trapped by his chest and thigh as well. He is ready for a few options, such as a foot lock, a knee bar, or a pass.

8

Across-side escape to reverse triangle

In this situation, Megaton is across-side on Royler and has his right arm between Royler's legs. The attacker may have his arm there to control your legs during the pass, or he may just place it there to control your hips. Whatever the case, as soon as you see it, you have an opportunity for a reverse triangle.

1 Megaton is across-side on Royler and has his right arm between Royler's legs.

Royler braces his left forearm in front of Megaton's neck, pushes off his left foot, and escapes his hips to his left. The brace in front of Megaton's head is essential; it keeps Megaton from following the hip escape and places his head in the perfect place for the move in step 3. Royler also blocks Megaton's left hip with his right forearm to keep Megaton from circling to Royler's head.

2

3 Royler wraps his left leg around Megaton's head as he pulls Megaton's right wrist with his left hand. Royler keeps blocking Megaton's left hip with his right hand.

Royler loops his right leg over his left foot, closing a figure-four reverse triangle on Megaton's right arm and head. Royler tightens his legs and pulls Megaton's right arm for choking pressure.

4

4 Detail

Note how Royler pulls Megaton's right arm toward his head to apply the triangle pressure on Megaton's neck. From this position, Royler can also change his hands and grab behind Megaton's left elbow, sliding his hand up to Megaton's left wrist and pulling the elbow down for an arm lock, or even apply a Kimura on Megaton's left arm.

Less dominant than the across-side position, the north-south position is generally used in submission grappling as a transition state when moving from one side to the other while across-side. The north-south, however, gives the attacker many submission options, as well as the chance to take the back, so it is important to know how to escape it. In this case, Royler's arms are inside Megaton's arms, so Royler chooses the pendulum escape. If his arms were outside, he would need to use the knees-through escape demonstrated in position 81.

1   Megaton is in the north-south position on Royler. Since his arms are inside of Megaton's arms, the first things Royler does are to brace his hands on Megaton's hips, hop his own hips down for distance, and stretch his legs out.

1 Detail

Note how Royler's arms are braced against Megaton's hips. It is very important to maintain the brace and the pressure of the arms throughout the entire move, otherwise the opponent will close back in.

2   Royler maintains the brace on Megaton's hips and starts to swing his legs from side to side, pushing off the opposite arm to create distance and power. First to his left...

3 Then down and around to his right. At every swing, Royler makes sure his legs are fully extended and his feet are low to the ground for the greatest leverage. If he swings his feet high rather than close to the ground, the circle will be shorter and the momentum generated will be much less. With each swing, Royler also pushes off, extending his arms and creating space between his torso and Megaton. Your opponent will know what you are up to, but as long as you keep the brace on his hips, there is little he can do. He may try to switch his hips, throwing his leg forward to the same side as you swing, but the swing movement is much quicker, making it very hard to follow.

Once he feels he has enough distance and momentum, Royler goes for the big swing, whipping his legs and head around with full force and coiling his inner leg (in this case his right leg as he swings to his right). The force of the legs in a pendulum are tremendous; if Megaton is not prepared, he may be reversed. **4**

5 Royler continues the rotation and drives his right knee all the way in to Megaton's left hip. With his right hand, Royler pushes Megaton's left elbow across so he can slip his right foot around the outside of Megaton's body.

Royler replaces the closed guard. **6**

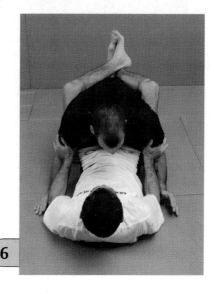

Obviously, the more options you have to escape any position, the more difficult you make it for your adversary to cover all the bases. As in position 80, Megaton is in the north-south position on Royler, but this time Royler's arms are on the outside, making it more difficult to use the pendulum method because he cannot brace Megaton's hips. (The method can still work, however, by leveraging your biceps instead.) Royler opts for the knees-through method of escaping and replacing the guard. The key to this method, again, is to use the brace to create and maintain space between you and your opponent.

1 Megaton is in the north-south position on Royler. Since Royler has his arms on the outside of Megaton's arms, he opts for the knee-through escape.

2 Royler bridges as he places his right forearm in front of Megaton's head.

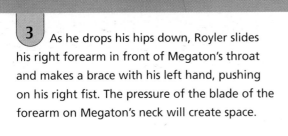

3 As he drops his hips down, Royler slides his right forearm in front of Megaton's throat and makes a brace with his left hand, pushing on his right fist. The pressure of the blade of the forearm on Megaton's neck will create space.

3 Detail

Note Royler's frame, with his right forearm in front of Megaton's throat and his left hand supporting his right wrist.

Royler slides his right knee under Megaton's right arm, creating more space.

4

5 Detail

Royler pushes Megaton's triceps forward, opening Megaton's arms, making it easy to slip his knees in.

5 Royler slides his left knee in as he changes his hands to prop under Megaton's armpits.

Pushing off his arms, Royler swings under Megaton as he kicks his left leg out and around the left side of Megaton's head.

6

7 Royler continues to spin to his left until his right knee comes out in front of Megaton's torso.

Royler swings his left leg over to the right side of Megaton and pushes his legs forward.

8

9 Royler replaces the guard.

Often in submission grappling matches, both fighters wind up on all fours, facing each other. This frequently happens as a defense to a guard pass, when the fighter being passed turns to his knees to avoid being scored upon. It is important to have some tools to get the opponent back down and secure the across-side position from which so many attacks originate.

1 Royler is on top of Megaton's back, both fighters facing each other. Notice that Royler puts the weight of his chest on Megaton's back to keep him pinned.

Royler runs to his left and wraps his right arm around Megaton's neck, still keeping his weight on Megaton's back.

2

3 Royler continues to move to his left until he grabs Megaton's left foot with his left hand and changes his right hand to grab Megaton's left elbow. At this point Royler's weight is still on Megaton's back, and he is dominating Megaton's left side.

Royler drives his chest forward on Megaton's side, pushing off his toes and toppling Megaton to his left. **4**

5 Royler secures across-side position, his right arm blocking Megaton's neck and his left blocking Megaton's hip.

Arm lock from all fours

As in position 82, we start with both fighters facing each other and Royler on top. Royler can't immediately force Megaton to the mat for control because this time he is farther away. Instead, Royler uses an alternative grip around Megaton's arm and goes directly for the submission. This grip around the arm is quite powerful and will work against even the most stubborn opponent.

1 Megaton is on all fours and tries to control Royler's legs.

2 Royler can't get his chest on Megaton's back to press him down and control him, so he wraps his right arm just under Megaton's left armpit and locks his fingers together, while pressing his left forearm into the back of Megaton's shoulder. Royler pulls his elbows together as if he were trying to touch one with the other.

2 Detail

Notice the grip: Royler's fingers are locked tight and his left forearm presses down on Megaton's left shoulder. Bringing his elbows together gives Royler greater leverage and tightness.

3 Royler turns Megaton over by lifting his right elbow while driving down with his left one as he drives his torso to his left.

Royler continues the pressure until he has Megaton's back on the mat. Note that Royler still has a lock on Megaton's left arm. **4**

5 Royler steps forward with his right leg, turns Megaton over to his left, and slides his left knee on top of Megaton's left hip.

Royler goes for the arm lock, sliding his hands to Megaton's left wrist and pulling it to his chest as he raises his hips, applying pressure to Megaton's left elbow. **6**

In this scenario, with both fighters facing each other, Megaton is able to shoot in and grab Royler's right leg with his right arm. If Royler doesn't react quickly, Megaton will grab his leg with both arms and be in a position to force him onto his back. Royler cleverly uses his legs to control Megaton's arm, and goes for a choke from the side.

Royler and Megaton are facing each other with Royler on top.   **1**

2   Megaton shoots forward and grabs Royler's right leg with his right arm. Royler sprawls to defend the leg hold, so Megaton can't lock in. Notice how Royler drives his hips down to force his leg back and break Megaton's grip. (If the sprawl is unsuccessful, you'll need to switch to the neck crank demonstrated in position 85.)

With Megaton still fighting to **3** gain the grip on his right leg, Royler circles to his left, wrapping his right arm around Megaton's throat and grabbing Megaton's left arm. Royler's left hand controls Megaton's left hip.

4 Royler switches his hips, shooting his right leg over the top and his left leg forward, trapping Megaton's arm with them. This lock applies a lot of pressure to the shoulder and sometimes to the elbow, depending on where the legs are in relation to the elbow.

Royler pushes his right arm further up **5** around Megaton's throat until he has his right elbow centered in front of Megaton's Adam's apple. He locks his right hand onto his left biceps, bends his left arm, locks his left hand on the back of Megaton's head, and sinks the choke. Notice that since Megaton's right arm is locked, he cannot use it to defend the choke. His left arm cannot help either, as it is the only brace supporting his body from hitting the mat.

5 Reverse Angle
Note Royler's leg position as he switches his hips. Royler shot his left leg forward and his right leg back, trapping Megaton's arm.

Neck crank from all fours

As in position 84, Megaton is able to shoot in and grab Royler's right leg. This time, however, Royler tries to sprawl, but sensing that he is losing the battle and will soon be toppled by Megaton, Royler employs an option to turn this bad situation into a submission opportunity.

1 Megaton has shot in and grabbed Royler's right leg.

2 Royler drops his chest on Megaton's back, opens his left leg, and reaches with his forearm in front of Megaton's head until he can grab Megaton's left wrist with his right hand. He also wraps his left arm around the inside of Megaton's left arm and locks in the grip near the elbow with his left hand.

3 Royler rolls forward over his left shoulder, kicking his left leg to help the roll. Royler then kicks his right leg over as well, driving Megaton over with him. (Notice that Royler's right leg pulls Megaton's right arm and upper body with it as he rolls.)

4 As he lands with his back on the mat, Royler closes a figure-four around Megaton's right arm and releases his left-hand grip on his own wrist.

Royler drives his legs down, forcing Megaton's hands to break open. He pulls Megaton's left arm back by the wrist with his right hand. **5**

6 Royler wraps his right arm above Megaton's left armpit and behind his head.

Royler pulls Megaton's head toward his head with both hands for a neck crank. **7**

Here is the counter to the lock demonstrated in position 83. As previously stated, that lock is very powerful, and if Royler doesn't react quickly, he will end up on his back in an arm lock. The key here is to react as soon as you feel the arm coming around your armpit and the hands locking over. If you allow the opponent to bring his elbows close together and apply pressure on your shoulder, it will be too late, because your head will be trapped on the wrong side for the escape to work.

1 Royler is on all fours and Megaton is able to wrap his right arm around Royler's left armpit and lock his hands together. Royler needs to react before Megaton can adjust his position and bring his elbows together, driving them down on Royler's back.

Royler steps back and out with his left leg, grabs Megaton's right triceps with his left hand, and shoots his head under the armpit. **2**

3 Bracing off his right hand and left foot, Royler shoots his right leg through as he pulls Megaton's right arm open and shoots his head up, driving it around Megaton's armpit and over the top of his shoulder. Notice how Royler's hips are pointing up and his buttocks are off the mat. He needs this clearance to keep his mobility as he goes for the next step.

Royler shoots his right leg over the top, pivoting over his left leg. **4**

5 Royler ends up in the reverse position on top of Megaton's back.

The next few moves demonstrate a series of attacks from the open guard. Royler likes to use the butterfly guard (guard with hooks inside) because it protects his feet and legs from submissions and gives him great mobility and many options. Perhaps his favorite move from the guard is this arm drag, which ends with Royler taking the back. The key to this move is the surprise of the arm drag and the hip slide to the side toward the back.

1 Royler has Megaton in his guard with hooks. He controls Megaton's wrists with both hands and keeps his hips distant from Megaton, looking for a lull in the action. Since Royler's hips are back, Megaton doesn't feel the threat of a sweep coming.

Royler quickly changes his right hand to Megaton's triceps. He leans back and pulls Megaton across his body by the right arm, left hand pulling Megaton's wrist and right hand dragging Megaton's elbow across. **2**

3 Royler continues to drive Megaton across his body as he sits up...

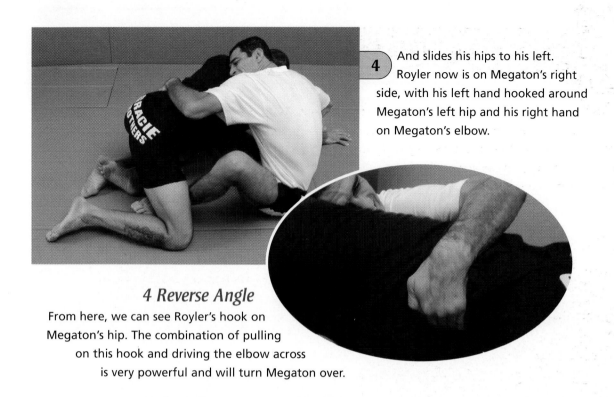

4 And slides his hips to his left. Royler now is on Megaton's right side, with his left hand hooked around Megaton's left hip and his right hand on Megaton's elbow.

4 Reverse Angle

From here, we can see Royler's hook on Megaton's hip. The combination of pulling on this hook and driving the elbow across is very powerful and will turn Megaton over.

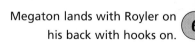

5 Royler releases his left foot and drives Megaton around, pushing his right elbow and pulling his left hip out, turning him onto his back.

Megaton lands with Royler on his back with hooks on. **6**

Sometimes during the butterfly-guard arm drag when you pull the opponent's right arm and try to cross it, he will resist by sitting back on his heels. If that happens, you need to change to the side arm bar shown here. The key to this technique is to make the hip escape pronounced enough to straighten the arm and give you enough space and angle to loop your leg over the opponent's head.

1   Royler has Megaton in his butterfly guard and is dominating both hands. Again, Royler is sitting with his hips far from Megaton and waits for Megaton to relax his guard.

2   Royler goes for the arm drag, grabbing behind Megaton's right elbow with his right hand as he sits back and attempts to pull Megaton's arm across his body. Megaton resists the move by bracing with his left arm and sitting back.

2 Detail
Notice Royler's grip, right hand grabbing around and behind Megaton's elbow. Since the elbow joint is a wide part of the arm, Royler's grip is secure and he can pull without his hand slipping—a key consideration when there is no gi.

3 Trapping Megaton's right arm under his armpit, Royler twists his torso to his right, leaning his head toward the mat as he releases his left foot and slides his hips left. Notice that Megaton does not fall all the way forward, as in the previous technique; he only leans forward, with his buttocks still close to his heels, but Royler's hip escape gives Royler the angle for the attack.

Continuing to twist his torso and head to the mat, Royler lifts Megaton's chin with his left hand as he starts to loop his left leg over it. **4**

5 Royler locks his left leg under Megaton's chin and turns his hips down as he straightens his body, applying pressure to the elbow.

In this technique, Royler again goes for the arm drag from the butterfly guard, but rather than take Megaton's back, he opts for the calf lock. This is a matter of personal choice or strategy. The calf-lock option is always there when the arm drag forces the opponent to fall forward, but many people prefer the security of taking the back (the surest move) to going for the submission, which gives the opponent a bigger chance of escape. A lot depends on the match situation; if you are significantly behind in points and time is running out, you should go for the submission.

1 Royler starts with Megaton in his butterfly guard while controlling both hands.

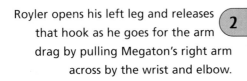 Royler opens his left leg and releases that hook as he goes for the arm **2** drag by pulling Megaton's right arm across by the wrist and elbow.

2 Detail
Note Royler's hand position during the arm drag. He crosses his hands to pull the arm across his hips.

3 Royler slips his right leg between Megaton's legs and wraps it around Megaton's right thigh, making sure his shin bone faces forward. Royler tightens the lock, pulling his right foot in with his left hand.

Royler grabs Megaton's right ankle and pulls it toward his head. **4** Although in this case Megaton's leg is up off the mat, Royler can get it even if it is lying flat.

5 Royler closes a figure-four with his legs, locking his left knee over his right foot as he continues pulling Megaton's foot toward his head for the calf lock.

5 Detail

Note how Royler crosses the figure-four, his leg just behind Megaton's knee, making sure the blade of his shin bone pushes on the calf for maximum pain.

The closed guard is the home of fewer submissions in submission grappling than in Brazilian jiu-jitsu. Because of the lack of cloth, most of the collar chokes that are so essential to opening up other possibilities from the closed guard are removed, leaving a much narrower range of options. This is one of those remaining options: Royler uses his hands and hips to pull Megaton forward, so he can wrap Megaton's arm for a different style of key lock.

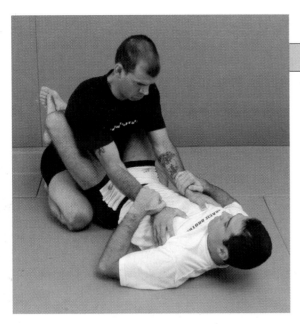

1   Royler has Megaton in his closed guard. Megaton is in good posture, back straight, head up, and hands on Royler's chest to maintain his base. The first thing Royler needs to do is to break Megaton's base. He cups his hands inside Megaton's wrists.

In one sudden motion, Royler pulls his hands out, taking away Megaton's brace, and brings his knees up toward his head, causing Megaton to fall forward. Royler circles his arms inside of Megaton's. **2**

3 Royler opens his legs and turns his hips to his right, putting his left heel on Megaton's right hip and hooking his right foot over Megaton's left leg while he continues to wrap Megaton's left arm with his right one, trapping it in his right armpit.

Royler completely wraps **4** Megaton's right arm with his forearm under the biceps/triceps area near the elbow. He locks his left hand over his right wrist. He applies the key lock by pulling up on his right arm as he leans back with his right shoulder. When applied correctly, this is a very tight lock and the opponent should submit quickly.

4 Detail
Note Royler's lock on Megaton's arm. For proper leverage, it is paramount that Royler trap the arm under his armpit and work his forearm under the biceps/triceps area.

Closed-guard arm bar

If, from the closed guard, you are unable to break your opponent's base, you need a technique other than the previous few. Here, Royler opens his guard, controls Megaton's elbow, and goes for the straight arm bar. An extra plus of this technique is that, if the opponent manages to twist his arm out to escape, you have the option to go for an omoplata.

1) Royler has Megaton inside his closed guard. He has tried to break Megaton's base without success.

Royler opens his legs and slides his hips to his left as he sticks his right arm inside Megaton's left arm and grabs behind Megaton's left elbow with his left hand. (2

3 Royler shifts his hips back and closes his guard, pulling Megaton's elbow with his left hand and helping to drive the arm up with his right arm. Royler's right arm is tightly wrapped around Megaton's arm and he opens his elbow, driving Megaton's wrist to his shoulder, where he will trap it with his head. At this point Megaton, anticipating the arm bar, may try to bend his arm and bring his left hand back toward his hips to evade Royler's head trap. If that happens, Royler will continue to move his head to his right, wrap his right leg around Megaton's left arm, and attempt an omoplata shoulder lock.

Royler opens the guard again and slips his hips to the right, placing his right knee on top of Megaton's right shoulder. He has trapped Megaton's right wrist between his head and his right shoulder and presses down on Megaton's elbow, pushing with his right hand and pulling with his left for the arm bar.

4

4 Reverse Angle

This view clearly shows Royler's hands applying downward pressure on the elbow, while his head locks in Megaton's left wrist. Notice Royler's right knee pressing down on Megaton's shoulder to help extend the arm.

The notorious biceps cutter is dangerous to both the recipient and the attacker. Because the lock is mostly a pressure pain against the muscle, people with great pain tolerance may resist it, and the result can be a nasty broken arm as the pressure on the bone builds. The attacker also needs to be careful when applying the lock. When he hooks his foot inside the opponent's arm, his lower leg is completely locked and his knee is vulnerable to being twisted should the opponent do a sudden move. Still, this is a popular and effective lock in submission grappling. The key is to "allow" your opponent to pass your guard as you lock in the biceps.

1 Royler has Megaton in his butterfly guard and is dominating both wrists.

2 Royler lies down on his right shoulder as he releases his left foot and hooks it under Megaton's right arm. He remains in control of both wrists and places his left shin in front of Megaton's right biceps. Notice that Royler lowers his right leg, giving Megaton a "free path" to pass the guard.

3 As Megaton passes to Royler's right, Royler continues to firmly control Megaton's right wrist and sits up slightly.

3 Reverse Angle

Note how Royler maintains control of Megaton's right wrist with his left hand as he reaches his right hand into the gap to grab behind Megaton's right arm.

With his right hand, Royler grabs Megaton's right triceps as he traps Megaton's forearm with his left leg. Royler makes sure he has the blade of his shin pushing against Megaton's biceps. This is the danger point for the attacker, whose left knee is very vulnerable to a twist.

4

5 Royler locks a figure-four around Megaton's right arm, right leg over his left foot as he uses both arms to pull on the back of Megaton's right arm, applying pressure with his shin to the biceps.

5 Detail

Note the blade of Royler's shin pressing in the biceps as Royler pulls Megaton's arm with both hands.

93

Open-guard behind-the-back Americana

This technique works well from both the open butterfly guard and the closed guard. It is used when you are battling your opponent for grip control, and quickly leads to a behind-the-back Americana lock. For some reason, this type of lock is not commonly used in submission grappling, which is all the more rea- son to use it: the technique works tremendously well and will surprise many an experienced fighter. The key to this technique is being able to control the grip and to use the power of your upper body sitting up to drive your opponent's arm back.

1 Royler is in the butterfly guard, controlling both of Megaton's arms by the wrists. Megaton tries to pull his hands back and out of Royler's grip. Royler opens Megaton's arms to prevent from pulling them close to generate power, or from grab- bing on to Royler's knee or hip to block the move.

Royler sits up, driving his head into Megaton's chest and using that forward momen- tum to push Megaton's right arm past his body. Royler reaches around with his right hand... **2**

3 And grabs Megaton's right wrist. At this point, Royler has both hands on Megaton's wrist and is in full control. Notice that Royler kept his hips back and just moved forward with his torso. This is important because when he sits back he wants to keep Megaton at a distance to prevent him from gaining the top.

Royler slides his left hand to Megaton's right elbow, still gripping Megaton's right wrist behind the back with his own right wrist, and starts to lie back on the mat. 4

5 Royler reaches over Megaton's right shoulder with his left hand, grabs Megaton's right wrist, and pulls the wrist up toward his head for the shoulder lock.

94

Open-guard triangle

As in position 93, this attack from the open guard starts with both opponents fighting for grip control. What you look for is the opportunity to explode your opponent's arms open and pull him forward. From there you can lock a triangle for the submission. This same technique can be used from the spider guard as well. The key here, once again, is speed and surprise.

1 Royler starts with Megaton in his guard with hooks controlling both wrists.

In one motion, Royler opens his right arm, pulls down on Megaton's right arm with his left hand as he releases his hooks, turns, and falls back to the mat, shooting his right leg between the arms over Megaton's left shoulder. Once Royler's right calf is on top of Megaton's back, he drives his heel down to the mat, forcing Megaton down with the leg.

2

3 As his back hits the mat, Royler's right leg is locked over the back of Megaton's neck, with his foot under his left knee in a figure-four. Royler drives Megaton's right arm across his body with his left hand.

Royler applies the choking pressure by pulling down on Megaton's head with both hands as he squeezes his knees together and down. 4

One of the most important closed-guard attacks is the Kimura, or shoulder lock. Opportunities for the Kimura happen frequently in submission grappling matches and need to be exploited, as they open up many other options. In the closed guard, when the opponent sits back to gain posture and you sit up to follow him, you have a few options: (1) if his head is forward, you can go for the guillotine; (2) if he is leaning too far back, you can turn to one side and shoot your hip over for the crossover sweep into the mount; and (3) if he counters the sweep by placing his hand on the mat to block you, you can lock a Kimura. In this case, Megaton is inside Royler's closed guard and has his left arm on the ground. This may have happened because he was blocking the sweep into the mount, or because he was pulled forward and braced with his arm. Regardless, every time your opponent has his arm there, the Kimura is open for you.

1 Royler has Megaton in his closed guard. Megaton has his left hand on the ground. Royler grabs Megaton's wrist with his right hand.

Royler opens his legs, pushes off his left foot to sit up, and crosses his left arm over the top of Megaton's left arm. **2**

3 Royler continues pushing off his left foot, raising his hips, and wraps his left arm around Megaton's left arm until his left hand locks onto his right wrist.

4 As he sits back, Royler pushes off his right toes, shifting his hips all the way across to his right, and drives Megaton's wrist up toward his head. Notice how far out Royler's hips are; this is important because he uses the power of the hip escape to drive the arm up. This will work against even the strongest of opponents.

Royler throws his right leg over the back to prevent Megaton from rolling forward to escape the pressure. His left leg blocks the front of Megaton's body to keep him from moving forward. Royler drives Megaton's wrist toward his right ear for the shoulder lock.

5

5 Detail
Note Royler's right leg over Megaton's back, blocking him from rolling forward. Royler's arms, interlocked with Megaton's left arm, drive the wrist toward the head.

96

Open-guard guillotine to overhead sweep to neck crank

This is one of Royler's bread-and-butter techniques. It is a guillotine turned overhead sweep turned neck crank. You can get into this position from many places, some of the most common of which are the butterfly guard (as the opponent leads with his head to push you back), the hook sweep (shown in position 97), and when the opponent is passing your guard. Regardless of the initiation point, the key is that the guillotine can occur at any point. You should attack it with the full intention of submitting your opponent. If he starts to defend by putting his weight forward, you sweep him overhead because the weight of his head is already leading him in that direction.

1 Royler has secured a guillotine choke on Megaton. Both his feet are inside Megaton's legs, acting as hooks. Megaton may have been attempting to pass Royler's guard, or may simply have been caught in the guillotine while in Royler's open or closed guard. Megaton leans forward to release some of the pressure on his neck.

1 Detail
Notice how Royler hooks his toes in to keep Megaton from circling his legs around and out of the hooks.

2 Using his hooks, Royler kicks his legs up and throws Megaton over his head.

3 Royler follows him over, landing in the mount with the guillotine still on.

4 Royler releases his hooks, shifts his weight to his right by extending his right leg and stepping forward with his left foot (because he has Megaton's neck wrapped by his right arm), and applies a neck crank by pulling Megaton's neck into Royler's right side.

97

Open-guard hook sweep

In addition to yielding a variety of submissions, the butterfly guard is also great for sweeps. The hook sweep is one of the most effective sweeps from the butterfly guard. The key is not to sit back and pull the opponent's body on top of you, but rather to escape your hips to the side and drive your head to the mat, sweeping the opponent in the direction of the arm that you have trapped so he cannot use it to block the sweep.

1 Royler has Megaton in his closed guard and opens his legs, placing both feet on the ground.

Pushing off his right foot, Royler escapes his hips to his right. **2**

3 Royler places his right foot between Megaton's legs, hooking under the left thigh.

Royler now escapes his hips to his left. **4**

6 Royler sits up, presses his head against the right side of Megaton's chest, and slides his right hand between Megaton's left arm and his torso. With his left hand, Royler pushes Megaton's right hand in close to his own body.

5 Royler hooks his left foot under Megaton's right thigh. He now has both hooks in and both hands controlling Megaton's wrists.

7 Royler will sweep to the side his head is on, using the weight of his head to assist in the motion. Since he has his head to Megaton's right, Royler sweeps in that direction. He moves his hips to his right and, leading with his head, he drives his left shoulder to the ground, pulls Megaton's right elbow around (keeping him from using his right arm to block the sweep), and raises his right leg, hooking under and lifting Megaton's left leg.

8 Royler continues the rotation, sweeping Megaton to his left.

9 Royler lands mounted.

98

Open-guard push-through sweep

Some positions are just too easy. Taking advantage of his opponent's reaction to a hook sweep attempt, Royler just pushes forward with his knee on the chest for a straight reversal. Make sure your knee is square in the opponent's chest and wait to act until he has pulled back from the sweep.

1 Royler has Megaton in his open guard and sets up the open-guard hook sweep, shifting his hips to his right and hooking his right foot on Megaton's left leg, with his head to Megaton's right. Royler has his right knee on Megaton's chest to have the push-through option ready, should Megaton lean back to escape the sweep.

As Royler pulls Megaton's right wrist and arm up for the hook sweep, Megaton reacts by leaning back. **2**

3 Royler follows Megaton's move and drives his right knee forward, pushing Megaton's chest and forcing him to lean farther back. Simultaneously, Royler pulls Megaton's right knee in with his left hand, taking away Megaton's last piece of base.

Royler continues driving his right knee forward into Megaton's chest, directing Megaton to the mat, and helps the motion with his right arm.

4

5 With his left arm, Royler pulls on Megaton's right elbow as he continues to drive his right knee forward, until he is across-side with his hips facing Megaton's head. Notice that at no time did Royler remove his right arm from between Megaton's left arm and torso, keeping inside control to the finish.

99

Open-guard sweep to the back

This is a great way to get to the back. Another one of the positions that uses misdirection, it stems from a reaction to the overhead sweep. As the defender sprawls and braces with his arms forward, you slide to the side and take the back.

Royler has Megaton in his butterfly guard, dominating both wrists, and opens Megaton's arms.

1

2 Royler scoots his buttocks forward and gets his left arm in between Megaton's right arm and body.

Royler opens Megaton's left arm, slides his right arm between Megaton's left arm and body, and locks his hands, gripping Megaton's chest tightly. His feet are hooked under Megaton's thighs and his buttocks are close in, knees bent to gain the most proximity.

3

3 Detail

Note how Royler locks his hands, pulling Megaton tight against his chest. He also has his feet hooked under Megaton's thighs and his hips almost under Megaton. Royler must be this close to be able to lift Megaton off the ground as he leans back. If Royler leaves any space, it will hurt his leverage because Megaton can shift his weight back to avoid being lifted.

Royler lies back on the mat as he pulls up on his arms, lifts his hooks, and throws Megaton over his head. Megaton reacts by stretching his body and bracing with both hands on the mat, blocking the sweep.

4

5 Royler pushes off his left leg and slides his body to his right as he releases the right foot hook, clearing a path to Megaton's back. (If your opponent prevents you from getting to the back by opening his legs to block your path, you can switch to the foot-lock submission demonstrated in position 100.) Notice how Royler claws Megaton's ribcage with his right hand to assist himself.

Royler gets to Megaton's back. **6**

In this position, Royler attempts to take the back using the previous technique, but Megaton defends by opening his legs, making it more difficult for Royler to get there. Royler immediately changes plans, grapevining his leg around Megaton's right leg and going for the foot lock.

Royler has his arms inside Megaton's arms and locks his hands, gripping Megaton's chest tightly. His feet are hooked under Megaton's thighs and his buttocks are close in, knees bent to gain the most proximity.

1

2 Royler lies back on the mat as he pulls up on his arms, lifts his hooks, and throws Megaton over his head. Megaton reacts by stretching his body and bracing with both hands on the mat, blocking the sweep. Royler braces his arms on Megaton's chest.

3 Royler attempts to go to the back, but Megaton opens his left leg to block the path. Royler keeps his arms bracing Megaton's chest and grapevines his right leg around Megaton's left one.

Placing his right foot on Megaton's left hip while pushing Megaton's torso to the left, Royler slides his own torso away. Notice that Royler has Megaton's left leg trapped by his right leg and body. He closes his left leg in to lock it even more. (If the opponent negates the leg trap by bending his leg, you should switch to the heel hook in position 102.) **4**

5 Royler locks his right arm around Megaton's left heel under the Achilles tendon, locking Megaton's foot with his right armpit, and stretches his body as he pushes Megaton's torso away with his right leg, applying pressure for the foot lock.

101

Open-guard sweep to the back to leg lock

This technique is very similar to the previous one; however, this time Royler goes for the knee bar instead of the foot lock. Both positions are equally effective. To a certain extent, your choice should depend on your opponent. The foot generally is easier to submit because it has weaker muscles, but some people have very flexible feet and can go a long way before submitting. The leg has bigger muscles and more power, but the knee has much less range of movement; therefore, the pain starts more quickly there.

Royler has his arms inside Megaton's **1** arms and locks his hands, gripping Megaton's chest tightly. His feet are hooked under Megaton's thighs.

2 Royler lies back on the mat, pulling up on his arms and lifting Megaton over his head. Megaton braces with both hands on the mat, blocking the sweep.

Royler attempts to go to the back, but **3** Megaton opens his left leg to block the path. Royler keeps his arms bracing Megaton's chest and grapevines his right leg around Megaton's left one.

4 Placing his right foot on Megaton's left hip while pushing Megaton's torso, Royler slides his own torso away. Notice that Royler has Megaton's left leg trapped by his right leg and body. He closes his left leg in to lock it even more. (If the opponent negates the leg trap by bending his leg, you should switch to the heel hook in position 102.)

Royler sits up and locks his right leg around Megaton's left knee, hooking his right foot under his own left leg and his left foot under Megaton's right knee, keeping Megaton from getting close or scooting to any side. Royler places his left hand and right elbow on Megaton's calf and shin to keep him from freeing his foot.

5

6 Royler applies pressure by straightening his legs. Pushing down on Megaton's left knee with his right leg at the same time that he straightens, driving the right foot down, adds pressure to the lock.

102

Open-guard sweep to the back to heel hook

As in the previous two positions, Royler attempts to take the back after the overhead sweep fails. This time, however, as he goes for a foot or knee lock, Megaton is able to bend his leg, negating those attacks. Royler quickly goes for the heel hook. This is another example of the sequences of moves or "phrases" that a submission grappler needs to have at the ready. The key is to be able to move seamlessly from one to the other as the opponent reacts.

1 Royler lies back on the mat and pulls up on his arms, lifting Megaton over his head. Megaton braces with both hands on the mat, blocking the sweep.

Royler attempts to go to the back, but Megaton opens his right leg to block the path. Royler keeps his arms bracing Megaton's chest and grapevines his left leg around Megaton's right one. 2

3 Placing his left foot on Megaton's right hip while pushing Megaton's torso to the right, Royler slides his own torso away.

Sensing the lock coming, Megaton bends his leg, negating the effort. Royler immediately wraps his left arm at the elbow around Megaton's right heel. **4**

5 Royler clasps his hands together, pushes off with his left foot, and twists Megaton's heel to the right for the heel hook. Notice that Royler's right foot remains hooked behind Megaton's left knee, keeping Megaton from rolling forward to avoid the pressure.

5 Detail
Notice Royler's grip on the heel, with his arm locking the heel at the elbow.

103

Open-guard foot sweep

Royler here demonstrates a great sweep from the open guard. Royler tries to pull Megaton forward and perhaps take his back. Megaton resists by leaning back and pulling his arm out, so Royler uses that reaction to sweep him.

1 Royler has Megaton in the traditional open guard, left foot on the right hip and right hook behind the left ankle. Royler starts the action by pulling Megaton's right arm toward him. Megaton reacts by leaning back as he tries to balance and pull his arm out. Royler pushes Megaton's hip back with his left foot as he pulls Megaton's left leg in with his right hook.

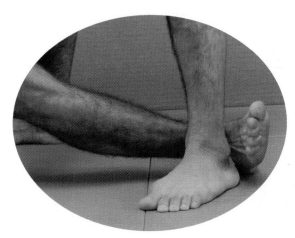

1 Detail A

Royler's right foot hooks right behind Megaton's left heel, greatly helping when he pulls the foot forward for the sweep.

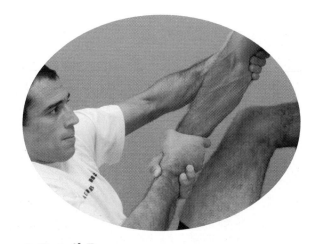

1 Detail B

Notice how Royler controls Megaton's right arm, right hand gripping the wrist and left hand grabbing the elbow for total control.

2 Royler quickly lets go of Megaton's arm and sits up, curling his right leg under his body. With his right hand, he grabs Megaton's left heel and continues to pull. Pulling with his left hand on the left knee helps force Megaton to the mat.

Bracing with his left foot, Royler continues pulling Megaton's left heel and switches his left hand to press down on the left knee until Megaton's buttocks hit the mat. **3**

4 Royler stands up, still in full control of the leg, with the same pull-and-push pressure, forcing Megaton all the way to the mat.

Conclusion

Submission grappling is a sport of great challenges and great rewards. The demands of the sport will not only greatly help you with your other grappling arts, but also further develop your understanding of the human body and mind. Although martial arts in general do wonders for self-confidence and self-esteem, because of its one-on-one nature, without the constraints of clothing or artificial rules, submission grappling epitomizes the human struggle for survival and superiority. Mastering the sport will give you a deeper connection to the warrior within. It will give you a sense of accomplishment that is hard to duplicate.

Ricardo Azoury photo